THE WATER BROUGHT US

The Water BROUGHT US

The Story of the Gullah-Speaking People

Muriel Miller Branch

Illustrated with photographs by Gabriel Kuperminc
and old prints

SANDLAPPER PUBLISHING CO., INC.

Dedication

This edition of *The Water Brought Us: The Story of the Gullah-Speaking People* is dedicated to Carrie Bell Brown and Janie Hunter who now reside with the ancestors.

===

ILLUSTRATION CREDITS:

Photographs courtesy of Avery Research Center for African American History and Culture, Charleston, S. C., pages 28, 72, 77 (right); Muriel Miller Branch, 11, 19, 23, 42, 68, 69; Willis Branch, 2, 60, 76, 80, 83, 85, 87; Katrinia Hamilton, 77 (left); Gabriel Kuperminc, 6, 21, 37, 40, 44, 45, 47, 71, 75, 81, 82, 88, 90, 91, 92, 94, 96; From Penn School Collection, Permission granted by Penn Center, Inc., St. Helena Island, S. C., 9, 29, 32, 33; South Caroliniana Library, University of South Carolina, Columbia, S. C., 13, 15, 25, 27, 38.

Library of Congress Cataloging-in-Publication Data

Branch, Muriel Miller.
    The water brought us: the story of the Gullah-speaking people / Muriel Miller Branch.
        p. cm.
    Includes bibliographical references (p.) and index.
    ISBN 0-525-65185-3
    ISBN 0-87844-153-0 pbk.
    1. Gullahs—History—Juvenile literature. I. Title.
E184.G84B73   1995
975.8'7—dc 20   94-49593   CIP   AC

First Paperback Edition, 2000
Second Printing, 2004
Published by Sandlapper Publishing Co., Inc.
Orangeburg, South Carolina 29115

Designed by Charlotte Staub
Printed in the United States of America

Acknowledgments

Until I sat beside Brent Ashabranner at lunch during a workshop at the University of Virginia, I was perfectly comfortable with the idea of collecting stories and developing learning centers on the Gullah culture for middle-school students. Brent never allowed me to return to that comfort zone. He coaxed, prodded, advised, and encouraged me through this entire project. A very special thanks to you, Brent.

I am deeply indebted to all of "my distant kin," the Gullah-speaking people of the Sea Islands who preserved their culture so that I might experience it. I am especially indebted to Carrie Bell Brown, Sam "Papa" Brown, Sadie Jenkins, Margaret Sumter, Gloria Wright, Janie Moore, Janie Hunter, Christina McNeil, Giffie and Bernie Brown, Yvonne Wilson, Bertha Stafford, and Emory Campbell for graciously sharing their stories, their culture, and, in several instances, their homes with an "outsider."

I am grateful for the love and forbearance of the four generations of family who share my home. The support of my husband, Willis; my mother, Missouri Miller; my two daughters, Cheryl and Sonja; and my four-year-old grandchild, Erica, has made the mammoth undertaking of writing and working full-time easier. My heartfelt thanks to friends, Emily Womack and Patricia Jones-Jackson, for accompanying me on the many trips to South Carolina. Thanks to Jerry and Connie Earl for the research they did and the valuable contacts they made for me in Columbia, South Carolina.

The staff of numerous school, public, academic, and special libraries and archives have been an invaluable help to me. I am particularly grateful to the staff at Penn Center, Avery Institute at the College of Charleston, South

Caroliniana Library at the University of South Carolina, Bon Air (Chesterfield) Public Library, Virginia State Library and Archives, National Museum of African Art, Richmond Public Library, University of Virginia, and Virginia Commonwealth University.

Contents

Waterfront development/condos and marina, Hilton Head Island, SC.

One

SEA ISLAND FOLKS

Stretching along the Atlantic Coast of South Carolina and Georgia in a long line are about thirty-five Sea Islands. Some of the islands are large; some are quite small. Several islands serve as wildlife preserves for endangered animals. A few, like Hilton Head and Kiawah, are famous for their resort developments. Others, like Cumberland Island on the Georgia-Florida border, are almost unknown to tourists. They have changed very little since before the Civil War. On most of these islands there live a people who call themselves Gullah and who speak a language with the same name. They are the descendants of slaves who toiled in the island fields and who stayed after Emancipation to become land owners, farmers, teachers, nurses, blacksmiths, doctors, and fishermen.

In many ways the Gullah are part of the modern world— they have luxury cars, big-screen televisions, cellular phones — but in other ways they have preserved the traditions of their ancestors. They weave beautiful baskets made of sweetgrass, bulrush, and pine needles. They tell stories about hags and haints (ghosts), the trickster Brer Rabbit, and the legendary John. They sing with equal passion old spirituals and modern gospel tunes. Their religious traditions and folklore have roots in Africa. Some Gullah-speaking people have left the Sea Islands for good; others have left and returned. Cousins Margaret Sumter and Sadie Jenkins are among those who worked for years "up north" and returned to their native St. Helena Island, South Carolina. Margaret returned after retirement, and Sadie returned to find employment on St. Helena after being retrained in nursing. Both women are now retired, and express a deep love for their home. For some Gullah families the tradition of island living has never been broken.

The Gullah story began to unfold for me in a restaurant overlooking the Ashley River in Charleston, South Carolina. The narrator was Janie Moore, a native of Yonges Island, South Carolina, who has lived most of her life in the Sea Island region. The setting provided a perfect backdrop for our meeting because Janie could point to the many historic landmarks as we talked.

Between bites of grilled cheese and sips of freshly squeezed Carolina lemonade, we talked about Gullah. Janie took her time to reflect on the questions I asked. It was as though she had protectively tucked Gullah memories away in a safe place in her mind. It took her a few moments to uncover them.

"Oh, yes!" she exclaimed at remembering some small detail that one of my many questions evoked.

The more Janie remembered, the more associations I was able to make of our mutual cultural traditions. Among the many traditions or superstitions which we shared, two stand out. Both of us were taught that everyone must be perfectly quiet during a thunderstorm because "God was doing His work." Then there was the superstition that it was bad luck to throw your hair outdoors because the birds might use it to build nests and cause you to have headaches. Janie and I took note of the cultural similarities and I wondered aloud if we might be distant kin. While I enjoyed sharing our common traditions and superstitions, I soon realized that the African traditions which had been retained or preserved in Janie's Gullah world had been lost in mine.

In the Petersville community of Yonges Island, South Carolina, where Janie Gilliard Moore grew up, many of the Gullah traditions are still practiced. Her family still speaks the Gullah language, and they still love to tell stories about life on the islands. Families are very close knit, often living in clusters of homes in the same neighborhood. One of the most intriguing features of Janie's neighborhood is how much it resembles an African village.

"You see, our houses are not in a line. The 'family home' has other houses just 'pop up' all around it, so that it looks like there is no order to it," Janie explained as we turned into the dirt driveway which encircled her community. As I drove along the common driveway which splinters off at each cluster of homes,

I could see clearly what she meant. The tin-roofed, weatherboard houses were scattered randomly around a big common yard.

"Africans who have visited here say that it looks and feels like their home," Janie said.

Then she told me about Michael Mawema, an African friend who visited the Sea Islands. She said that he was so struck by the similarities in customs that he exclaimed, "Janie, you are pure African!"

Janie was flattered by his comments, for like many other Gullah-speaking people, she is proud of the cultural link between herself and Africans. However, she says that it wasn't until she visited Nigeria as a part of the International Women's Conference that she fully understood the relationship between West Africans and the Sea Islanders.

"I am a Sea Islander who for many years did not recognize that my religious practices, beliefs, and customs — so many things, in fact, that made up my very being — were African."

But Janie has not always been proud to be Gullah. "When I was in school, I was made to feel bad. We were called backward folks, ignorant folks. We were teased and no one wanted to be associated with us. Even our teachers tried to browbeat us out of speaking Gullah," Janie recalls.

Today, however, Janie Moore, who holds a Master of Sacred Theology degree from Interdenominational Theological Seminary, realizes the importance of her heritage. Returning to Yonges Island after graduation from the seminary, Janie dedicated herself to improving the conditions of her people.

"I wrote a proposal and was awarded a $3 million grant from the Farmers Home Administration to bring indoor plumbing and add bathrooms to the homes in my community. Our children were getting sick and everyone was wondering why. I knew why. The water was contaminated from feces and other waste," she explained.

Janie confesses that it was a sacrifice to come back home, but when she sees the bathrooms added onto each of the homes in her community, she knows she made the right decision.

𝒥anie Hunter, a renowned storyteller and folklorist, stepped into the circle of light on the stage of the beautiful Wheelwright Auditorium on the campus of USC Coastal Carolina College, and a hush went over the audience. We waited in breathless silence as she stood alone in the white light for a brief moment. Then a thunderous applause went up, and we sprang to our feet in admiration of the Sea Island woman who has spent most of her adult life passing on her Gullah culture through stories and songs.

"My mother and father asked me to keep the stories and songs and pass them on as I travel through the world," she once told author-storyteller Marian Barnes.

For more than thirty years, the very spiritual and humble Johns Island native has been carrying out her parents' wishes by sharing the stories and folktales, and singing the songs that they taught her when she was a little girl. Today, the mother of fourteen children and grandmother of over one hundred and fifty, is passing those stories on to her children, grandchildren, and to the

Janie Hunter and her daughter "Tina" in concert.

nation. She is determined that the flame which was lit so long ago by her ancestors will not go out.

"I'm not ashamed of who I am," she proudly proclaimed to the crowd of about three hundred people who packed Wheelwright Auditorium at the Awards Night Concert sponsored by the National Festival of Black Storytelling in Myrtle Beach, South Carolina. "That's why I'm passing the Gullah stories and songs on to my children and my grandchildren," she declared in her thick Gullah accent. "And every Sunday after church my family get together, and me and Tina (her daughter) teach the children about our culture," says the Sea Island griot. (Griot, the European word for the African word "gewel," is a storyteller and historian. In the African and African-American tradition, the griot is the most important storyteller in the community, a revered person who is entrusted with passing down the cultural history of a people through stories and songs.)

Mrs. Hunter was being honored at the Festival for her contributions to storytelling. Joined on stage by two of her daughters, the trio brought the audience to its feet with their animated renditions of spirituals in Gullah.

Another contemporary Sea Islander is Emory Campbell. A native of Hilton Head Island, South Carolina, he is an activist who for years has fought to preserve the Gullah culture and lands. He has worked tirelessly to keep land in the hands of African Americans who obtained it during and immediately after the Civil War.

Often coming up against resort developers, the wiry Emory Campbell stands his ground and speaks his mind. "Developers just come in and roll over whoever is there. [They] move them out or roll over them and change their culture, change their way of life, destroy the environment, and therefore the culture has to be changed," he charged in a 1982 interview with Vernie Singleton, a life-long resident of Hilton Head Island and a free-lance writer.

In 1989, Emory Campbell was interviewed by Morley Safer of "60 Minutes." The broadcast drew national attention to the harmful effects of resort development on the African-American community of Hilton Head Island. The program also called attention to the living conditions of African Americans, the outrageous taxes they were expected to pay on mere shanties, and the limited number of high-paying jobs resort development brought to the native people.

But fighting land developers is only a part of what Emory Campbell does. As Executive Director of Penn Center on St. Helena Island, South Carolina, the oldest school for freed slaves in America, he is in charge of all educational programs as well as community service and self-help projects that affect Sea Islanders. He also manages the York W. Bailey Museum, named for the first African-American doctor on St. Helena Island. Housed in one of the oldest buildings at the Penn Center, the York W. Bailey Museum has the largest collection anywhere in the country of original papers, pictures, clothing, and artifacts representing the Sea Island culture.

Mr. Campbell is a firm believer in the importance of family and self-help. He encourages families to form coalitions to retain and develop the land that their forebears worked to purchase. "We have to establish them [opportunities] ourselves, for ourselves, our community, and children to come," Emory Campbell advises.

Gullah is both language and people. It refers to the approximately 150,000 Gullah-speaking African Americans who make their homes along the southeastern coast of South Carolina and Georgia, but it also refers to the Creole language their ancestors created and which they still speak. Gullah (or Geechee as it is called in Georgia) is considered a Creole language because it is a mixture of English and languages spoken along the West African coast. It came about because Africans from different tribal and language backgrounds needed to communicate. Some historians believe that the word Gullah originated from the word Angola, the West African country from which so many Africans were imported. Others, like the African-American linguist, Lorenzo D. Turner, attributes the word Gullah to Gola, a small tribe on the Sierra Leone-Liberia border where the Mende and Vai territories come together. The word "Geechee" seems to come from the pronunciation of Kisee (pronounced geezee), an African tribe which lived in an area adjoining Sierra Leone, West Africa.

African Americans who live on the Sea Islands (a string of about thirty-five islands extending from Pawleys Island near Myrtle Beach, South Carolina, to

Dr. York W. Bailey — first African-American doctor on St. Helena Island, SC.

Amelia Island on the Georgia-Florida border) are the descendants of enslaved Africans. They were brought to South Carolina and Georgia from Barbados in the West Indies and later from West Africa. African slaves of the Sea Islands created for themselves a culture that helped them survive in their new environment.

The isolation of one Sea Island from another and from the mainland has enabled the Gullah-speaking people to preserve their language, and maintain many of their ancestral customs in a manner that makes them the most "authentic" Americans of African descent.

Janie Moore summed up the uniqueness of today's Gullah-speaking people in one sentence, "We are a living museum."

In the pages ahead we will explore the "living museum" of the Sea Islands, but to understand better the Gullah-speaking people of today we must first look at the past out of which they came.

Two

WHEN TIMES WERE HARD:
Slavery in the Low Country

*T*he European castles which dotted the 1,500 miles of West African coastline during the seventeenth and eighteenth centuries were not the grand and festive palaces of kings and queens. Instead, they were fortresses which had been built by the Portuguese in the fifteenth and sixteenth centuries as trading centers. During the African slave trade, they became the places where African princes, princesses, peasants, and prisoners, bound by massive concrete and stone walls, all shared the same fate — bondage. They were places where the sorrowful moans and wails of newly imprisoned Africans, who had been wrenched from their families and villages, drowned out the familiar sounds of waves crashing against ebony lava rocks. They were places where hungry, tired, and frightened Africans waited in dark, poorly ventilated cells to be loaded on slave ships for the long and horrifying trip across the Atlantic Ocean.

Behind the masses of concrete, captive Africans were chained to strangers from other West African tribes to avoid uprisings. Thousands of them had been marched hundreds of miles to the coast from the interior of Senegal and other West African countries, or forced at gunpoint onto small boats and rowed down the Congo, Niger, and Gambia rivers to wait until the slave ships were ready to sail.

These castles, then, were really slave warehouses. They also served as headquarters for American and European slave merchants and agents who made deals and traded goods for humans in the same way they traded cattle or cotton. Slaves were a commodity which brought them huge profits. So much so, that by the eighteenth century, large companies were being formed for the sole purpose of supplying the demand for slave labor.

One of the most infamous slave trading companies was the Royal African Company which owned and operated 249 slave ships. Slave ships which had been given names like *Jesus, John the Baptist, Liberty,* and *Brotherhood* cruised the West African coast, collecting their human cargo, and engaging in the cruelest of all trade — people. Their shopping lists included jet black, large, tall, strong, healthy African males between the ages of eighteen and twenty-five or healthy

Old Slave Mart Museum, Charleston, SC, the site where slaves were held and auctioned.

African women between the ages of fourteen and eighteen. Darker-skinned Africans brought premium prices in the slave market because they tended to be stronger, healthier, and tolerated heat better than the lighter-skinned ones.

Many slave castles and forts were built with the consent of the local African rulers in exchange for guns, money, and goods. Africans who were most likely to be kept in these dungeons were those who had been captured during battles between tribes. Africans fought each other for land and power just like all other peoples. The conquerors frequently took their captives as bounty and forced them into slavery.

Ports such as Gorée Island, Senegal, and Bunce Island, Sierra Leone, were important stopovers on what became the Triangular Trade or Middle Passage. It was from these slave-trading ports that Africans were brought to the Sea Islands. The Triangular Trade route actually began in the West Indies where ships were loaded with sugar and molasses. From the West Indies, the loaded ships sailed to Massachusetts where the sugar and molasses were traded for rum, guns, and cloth. These products would in turn be taken to West Africa where they would be exchanged or traded for Africans.

During the early days of slavery, Africans were taken first to Barbados, Jamaica, and other West Indian countries to be "broken in" or to work on the huge sugar plantations. They were beaten, denied food, and humiliated until they appeared tame and obedient to the slave trainer's every demand. Then, they were shipped to Charleston, South Carolina; Norfolk, Virginia; or other slave-trading ports in America to be sold. This heartless trade, named for the shape of the route, operated for over two hundred years before it was outlawed by Congress in 1808.

Frequently, slave ships, many of which were converted cattle ships, sailed with five hundred or more Africans when they were only designed to hold two hundred. Men, women, and children were packed in tiny compartments like chickens in cages. Some stalls were so small that the captives had to crawl to get inside. Some of the most ruthless captains made the enslaved Africans lie down breast to back in compartments large enough for only one person, making any movement almost impossible. Added to their misery, they were often forced

"Slave Sale," Charleston, SC.

to sit or lie for days in their own feces, urine, and vomit because they were unable to move. Numerous slaves became sick and died because of these unsanitary conditions. Author-historian Vincent Harding described the slave ships as "kennels where human beings were forced to exist for weeks and months in conditions not fit for animals."

Conditions on the "slavers" were so horrible that many African captives plotted with their shackled partners to commit suicide, preferring death over slavery. Suicide took many forms, but the most common was to jump from the ship into the shark-infested Atlantic. Open rebellion against captains or overseers was another form. Some slaves refused to eat or drink even after being beaten almost to death for refusing to do so. Others simply willed death, and, since they believed in the hereafter, they felt that their souls would go back to Africa. These uprisings at sea were the forerunners to numerous rebellions which would later take place in America.

An estimated 20 million Africans were shipped from Gorée Island, Senegal, during the height of the slave trade because Gorée Island and Bance (later named Bunce Island), Sierra Leone, were two of the major slave-trading ports in West Africa. Why these two countries? Many theories have been given. One theory is that Africans from the Senegal and Gambia region were highly skilled farmers, fishermen, miners, and artisans, thus making them a valuable free labor source for the expanding rice, cotton, and indigo plantations in America.

Rice was a new, booming business in pre-Civil War South Carolina. Therefore, planters needed the know-how of the Africans who had years of experience in cultivating it. The figures on the number of slaves brought from West Africa seem to support this theory because 43 percent of all Africans brought to South Carolina during the eighteenth century came from Senegal, Gambia, Angola, and Sierre Leone where rice was an important crop.

As one slave owner put it, "Africans were more than familiar with the rice crop, they were familiar with the *cultivation* of the crop." Thus, Africans from rice-growing regions were very highly valued, and played a major role in establishing the immensely profitable Sea Island rice plantations.

Africans who had just arrived in the Charleston area probably saw a lot that was familiar. The blue waters of the Atlantic Ocean lapping at the jagged shorelines, the inlets and intracoastal waterways weaving their way between islands, the busy Charleston Bay, and the smell of the salty marshes must have reminded them of their own homeland. Surely they recognized the giant wafflelike rice fields which stretched out along the Ashley, Santee, and Cooper rivers.

As the number of imported slaves increased, so did the wealth of the slave owners. According to the 1860 U.S. census, there were only eighty-eight slave holders in the United States who owned more than three hundred slaves. Of that number, twenty-nine owned rice plantations in South Carolina. Of the fourteen slave holders who owned more than five hundred slaves, nine of them lived in South Carolina.

The slave culture of the Sea Islands was different from slave cultures in other

"Harvesting Rice"

parts of South Carolina and Georgia for several reasons. The tremendous size of the rice plantations along with the huge amount of labor it took to raise and harvest rice led to the development of a different type of labor system. The "task" system of dividing work among slaves was created on the rice plantations in South Carolina to take care of the endless and demanding work of growing rice. Coal black men cleared acres of trees from the land. The average task for a slave who cleared the land was 1,200 square feet a day. Slaves also dug miles of trenches or ditches with simple tools like spades and hoes. They plowed and pulverized the ground to get it ready for planting. Slaves built huge banks or dams to hold the water in the rice fields. Women were assigned the task of planting at least a fourth of an acre of rice each day. To the rhythm of work songs, they dropped the seeds and covered them with their quick feet. They also chopped weeds from the rice fields so that the tender plants would not be choked out. Slaves were assigned the job of letting water in and out of the fields at just the right time. There were slaves who did nothing but repair the banks to keep them from leaking and flooding the plants at the wrong time.

Tasks or jobs, which were calculated to last all day, were assigned each morning by the owner. Under the task system, the overseer got his orders from the owner. The "slave driver," who was himself a slave and who served as a foreman, took his orders from the overseer. Every day, the slave driver assigned tasks to each slave, and he was responsible for insuring that they completed all of their work.

The task system, then, seemed to have given slaves of the Sea Islands a sense of independence, a sense of personal contribution and ownership, and an attachment to the land that slaves inland did not have. Slaves of the "low country" took pride in having created prosperous plantations out of wilderness and marshland with their labor, their skill, and, yes, their loyalty. A former slave, Gabe Lance, remarked, "All dem rice field been nothing but swamp. Slavery people cut kennel [canal] and cut down woods—and dig ditch through raw woods. All been clear up for plant rice by slavery."

Slaves seemed to tolerate the heat and diseases carried by insects, particularly mosquitoes, much better than their European masters. So, during the "sickly months," which lasted from April to October, planters and their families took refuge in villages and towns such as Charleston to escape the unfriendly environment and illnesses which ravaged the "low country." Fear of getting malaria was so great that most planters were afraid to spend a single night in the rice field country. In many instances even the overseer would not stay on the plantation. Consequently, slaves were left alone to manage the huge plantations by themselves. The practice of leaving the slaves to manage themselves and the crops for long periods of time gave the African slaves of the Sea Islands a sense of independence. It also allowed them to practice their cultural traditions without the fear of interference from an unsympathetic overseer or owner.

Isolation of the plantations from other islands and the mainland, and the large number of slaves from the same regions of West Africa, played a big part in the rise of the unique slave culture of the Sea Islands. Furthermore, Sea Island slaves were very likely to stay with the same "family" or owner for generations because their knowledge of rice cultivation was so greatly needed. Hence, Sea Island slaves developed a fierce sense of ownership in the plantation.

The story is told about a former slave named Morris who got word that the new superintendent of the plantation planned to put him off the plantation because he was old. Word had gotten around that the superintendent considered old Morris lazy and "no count." When Morris heard about it, he went to Mr. Baruch, the owner, and said, "I was born on dis place, and I ain't agoin' off. I was born on dis place before Freedom. My Mammy and Daddy worked de rice fields. Dey's buried here. De fust ting I remember are dose rice banks. I growed up in dem from dat high ... De strentht of dese arms and legs and of dis old back, Mist' Bernie, is in your rice banks." He finished by declaring, "No, Mist' Bernie, you ain't agoin to run old Morris off dis place." Morris stayed.

The Sea Island slave's desire to be free was uppermost in his mind. He brought with him memories of the slave castles and the horrid Middle Passage, of seeing brave men and women jump to their deaths in the name of freedom, or witnessing captives being hanged from the ship's masthead or being shot to death for rising up against the captain. He carried that same longing for freedom in his own heart.

Resistance to slavery increased greatly among Sea Island slaves during the early nineteenth century. They resisted in secret and subtle ways, and they resisted in open and daring ways. Some of the most common rebellions were work slowdowns, setting fires to buildings and crops, and breaking work tools such as hoes. The more drastic rebellions included stealing food, poisonings, and deserting the plantation. Occasionally, a slave would refuse to be pushed any further or worked any harder by his or her master. One Sea Island slave threatened to drown herself if her master forced her to work any harder than she was working already. Fearing that she might just follow through on her threat, her master gave in.

Slave rebellions, large and small, claimed hundreds of thousands of lives in the Americas. In South Carolina alone, hundreds of slaves were killed in uprisings. Approximately one hundred slaves were killed or executed for their participation in the Stono Rebellion. Thirty-five were killed for plotting an uprising in Charleston in 1822. Eighteen more slaves lost their lives at Dunbar Creek on St. Simons Island, Georgia, but for each life that was lost in rebellions, there were an equal number rising up elsewhere to protest the unfair system of slavery.

One of the best illustrations of unity among rebel slaves is told by the famous Gullah folklorists Doug and Frankie Quimby. They tell the true story of eighteen African men of the Ibo tribe who made a pact to die rather than be enslaved. They linked themselves together and waded into Dunbar Creek, shouting, "Water brought us, and water's gonna take us away." This site is known today as Ibo Landing. It is located on St. Simons Island, Georgia. The slave rebellion at Ibo Landing is said to be the origin of the famous Negro spiritual, "Oh, Freedom."

I didn't know a thing about the Stono Rebellion until Janie Moore, a Sea Islander, told me about it. She rode with me about twenty miles outside of Charleston to show me the site of the rebellion. We got out of the car, and Janie squeezed through the opening in the closed gate. She beckoned for me to join her. She waved one hand to scatter the swarm of gnats which rose up out of the warm, tall grass, and, with her free hand, she shielded her eyes against the sun. Janie peered across the field to find the historical marker which was to have been placed at the site some time ago. She was clearly disappointed that it had not yet been placed there.

"There should be an historical marker here," she said. We walked toward the barn which was within sight of the river where the Stono Rebellion began. Standing in the midst of a huge field overlooking the water, Janie told me the story of the rebel slaves and their quest for freedom.

"This is where some Sea Island slaves began their rebellion back in 1739. They were trying to escape to Florida," she began. "None of the tours would ever have brought you out here just like they didn't take you by the Emmanuel A. M.

E. Methodist Church where Denmark Vesey planned his uprising," she added. Denmark Vesey was a free black Charlestonian who purchased his freedom with a large sum of money he won in a lottery. The site of the Stono Rebellion of 1739 is now the home of an African-American Farm Cooperative, but the memory of the rebellion is as fresh in Janie's mind as if she had actually been there to witness it.

The Stono Rebellion took place in St. Paul's Parish, near the western part of

Plaque, National Historic Landmark, commemorating the Stono Slave Rebellion. Plaque held by Felder Freeman, Ravenel, SC.

the Stono River, which is about twenty miles from Charleston. On a Sunday morning in September, 1739, a slave named Jemmy led about twenty of his fellow slaves in a revolt against their masters. These rebels for freedom marched through South Carolina on their way to Spanish-occupied St. Augustine, Florida, defiantly beating their drums, carrying a flag, and calling out, "Liberty!" As they marched, other slaves joined their ranks.

Sounding the drums proved to be a deadly decision for the rebels, but it was also an open sign of defiance which seemed to have been common among black insurrection leaders. Vincent Harding believes that the beating of drums made the marchers feel like African warriors again. Late that Sunday afternoon, the band of about one hundred slaves was stopped by the militia, but not before they had burned and ransacked houses and barns and had killed almost every white person in their path.

In July, 1822, Denmark Vesey organized an elaborate plan to free thousands of slaves in Charleston and the surrounding Sea Islands. He, "Gullah Jack" Pritchard, Rolla Bennet, Monday Gell, and Ned and Peter Poyas began meeting with members of the black community in Vesey's home, at religious gatherings on plantations, and outside slave cabins to plan a revolt. They used the unrest that the slaves felt at being kicked out of the white church to get slaves to rally behind them. Each group of slaves was given specific responsibilities. For example, blacksmiths were to make bayonets and spikes. Men who cared for horses were to get the horses. Still other slaves were to get fuses and gunpowder. Each group's contribution was important to the plan.

Unfortunately, Vesey and his friends were betrayed by a slave who told his master about the plot. Over a hundred slaves were arrested, and Vesey and thirty-four others were executed. Uprisings among Sea Island slaves were so prevalent during the late eighteenth and early nineteenth centuries that modern historians have dubbed them "The Gullah War."

The fear of betrayal, torture, or death did not keep enslaved Africans from trying to break free. Though not as well documented as the uprisings and rebellions at Stono, Charleston, or Ibo's Landing, thousands of individual slaves resisted slavery — acting out their own personal yearning for freedom.

Emmanuel A.M.E. Methodist Church, Site of Denmark Vesey's planned insurrection.

Three
BEYOND FREEDOM

$\mathcal{C}$annonballs, like large black eyeballs, are still embedded in the sandy soil of the Sea Islands. Once in a while one surfaces as a reminder of battles fought on the islands. The trail of blackness in the flaxen sand are relics of the Civil War which began at Fort Sumter, South Carolina, on April 12, 1861. The "gun shoot" at Bay Point, located at Port Royal Sound at Hilton Head, South Carolina, began less than six months after Confederate forces fired the first cannon on Fort Sumter.

Several days prior to the "gun shoot," Union Navy ships gathered in Port Royal Sound. The ships were watched nervously by Confederate forces who hoped that they would soon move on. But, on November 7, 1861, their hopes were dashed as Union ships moved defiantly farther and farther into their territory. By early afternoon, the Confederate flag was brought down and the Sea Islands of Port Royal, St. Helena, and Hilton Head changed from Confederate to Union strongholds.

The "gun shoot at Bay Point," as the slaves called it, brought about rapid and dramatic changes in the lives of Sea Island residents, slaves and slave owners alike. Before November 7, neither slave nor slave owner could have imagined that the Sea Islands would undergo Reconstruction before the Civil War was over. Nor could either imagine that they would lead the South, or the nation, in its Reconstruction efforts. As unlikely as it may have seemed, the Sea Islands did become the leader in the Reconstruction movement. It was here in coastal South Carolina that the first slaves were recruited to prove that they were capable of serving in the Army.

It was on the Sea Islands that the first schools for former slaves were estab-

Civil War cannon, Charleston, SC.

lished and an all-out assault on illiteracy began. The Sea Islands are where the first abandoned land was taken and given or sold to freedmen. It was here also that the wage system for former slaves was first tested. Slaves on the Sea Islands were the first to bargain for better working conditions and pay. And it was here, in the Confederate state of South Carolina, that local and state politics opened up for men like the famous skipper, Robert Smalls, who commandeered his master's ship *The Planter* and piloted it into Union territory.

But that first volley of gunfire between Union and Confederate forces meant different things to slaves and slave masters. Slaves heard it as a welcome blast for freedom and they rejoiced openly. Slave owners heard it as a signal to take at least temporary refuge in safer places inland.

The word of Union occupation spread rapidly among the slaves who streamed in from the fields to find their masters hastily loading their families and belongings on flatboats in preparation to leave the islands. Therefore, one of the first changes to take place was the relationship between the slaves and their masters. A major twist was that, for the first time, slaves were in a position to say *no*, which many of them did when their masters demanded that they go inland with them. It was a response that a few hours earlier would have resulted in a corrective "flogging."

The plight of the newly freed slaves became a concern for the Federal government and abolitionists who hoped to use the Port Royal situation to prove that the emancipation of slaves would benefit all. As a result, Secretary of War William Stanton sent Edward Pierce, a young Boston lawyer and abolitionist, to Port Royal to come up with a plan to deal with the problem. Under Pierce's plan, missionaries would be sent to take care of the religious needs of the newly liberated slaves. Teachers would be sent to instruct them in reading, writing, and arithmetic. Superintendents would be sent to manage the plantations. Plantations were to be run by the government under the direction of the superintendents.

As the war escalated, slaves joined the Union ranks for safety and freedom, creating a massive problem for the military leaders at Port Royal. What could they do with so many newly released men and women who were neither slave nor free? First they had to take care of their immediate needs for food, clothing, and shelter. Then they used the skills of this multitude of refugees to take care of their own overwhelming need for manpower. Refugees were put to work on fortifications, supply lines, and in personal service in the Union camps. They also worked as scouts, spies, guides, cooks, and blacksmiths.

Insuring the safety of fugitive slaves was first enforced by General Benjamin Butler at Fortress Monroe, Virginia, in the spring of 1861 when he refused to return fugitive slaves to their owners. He was also the first to recognize just how important slave labor was to the Confederate war effort. Therefore, Butler concluded that, "Slave property, like any other property, might rightfully be appropriated by the army upon grounds of military necessity, especially when such property was being employed in the enemy's cause." From that point on, the Union army began confiscating slaves with other property, and using their labor to help them win the war. Slaves became contraband and could be seized by the government as easily as food, oxen, cotton, houses, and land.

Providing a place of safety for the newly released slaves behind Union lines presented other problems. Could or should former slaves be armed to fight the rebel Confederates? How would their enlistment affect their freedom? These questions were as hotly debated in the North as they were in the South. Military leaders, political leaders, and abolitionists were at odds over the status of the newly liberated Negro man who was drafted or who volunteered for the army.

Two laws were passed in 1862 which guaranteed that ex-slaves and free blacks who fought in the Union army and navy would be free. The first Act of March 13, 1862, prohibited the return of fugitive slaves by military officers. The Militia Act of July 17, 1862, contained a clause which had an even greater bearing on Sea Island men because it provided that slaves who rendered military service would be free. Not only would they be free, but their families would be free also. This marked another turning point for many former Sea Island soldiers

Dress Review of First Regiment, South Carolina (Negro) Volunteers, Hilton Head, SC.

who were able to guarantee freedom for their families with their military service. For the first time, the African-American male of the Sea Islands could enjoy his role of having authority over the fate of his family.

Abandoned Sea Island plantations caused an even more complex problem for the Federal government. Who was entitled to the land? How much land would former slaves be entitled to purchase or be given? Who was going to work the much needed cotton crops to bring in money? Answers to these questions did not come easily. To make matters worse, Yankee leaders knew nothing about the slave culture and even less about farming. Consequently, they were unable to provide the leadership needed to make cotton "King" as it had been during slavery.

Changes in the makeup of the population of the Sea Islands quickly followed the "gun shoot." Before the nozzles of the cannons cooled from that first battle, planters and their families were fleeing the islands for safer places. Many of the men and boys left to join the Confederate army, reducing the white population to almost nothing. The exodus of whites was so complete that General Sherman made a public appeal to them to stay and accept the protection of Federal forces. He tried to assure them that he didn't intend to interfere with their "social and local institutions." They were not convinced.

White Sea Island residents were soon replaced by Northern abolitionists, philanthropists, missionaries, fortune-seekers, military personnel, ministers, cotton agents, superintendents. However, released slaves still accounted for the greatest increase in the population of the area as they sought sanctuary within Union lines.

Each group of newcomers had a personal stake in the fate of the newly liberated Negro. Philanthropists saw it as a chance to give to the worthy cause of the helpless Negro. Missionaries saw it as an opportunity to convert "lost" souls. Fortune-seekers seized the chance to swallow up large parcels of land and to find ways to fill the pockets of Northern merchants. Military leaders needed able-bodied men to serve in the war. Teachers saw a chance to teach eager Negro children and adults to read and write. Finally, the abolitionists saw Port Royal as an incubator for a social change which became known as the Port Royal Experiment.

In the meantime, released slaves tried to make sense of their own tentative

King cotton.

freedom. They recognized almost immediately that the change in their status did not necessarily work to their advantage. Many of them were without adequate food because Union soldiers helped themselves to the food they found in abandoned homes and storehouses. They were without adequate clothing because clothes were usually rationed out to them around Christmas.

One of the strongest principles of the Port Royal Experiment, which began in 1862, was that of self-help and industry. Missionaries were given the responsibility of teaching the Negroes civilization, Christianity, industry, economy, self-reliance, and inspiring them with self-respect. Former slaves were told that faithful work was expected from them and they could expect good care, justice, and instruction in reading from the missionaries.

Faithful work included cultivating the fine Sea Island cotton which was in high demand. The high quality textiles which were made from the silky Sea Island cotton made it more desirable and more expensive than other types of cotton. Because of the high market value of Sea Island cotton, cotton agents, missionaries and others tried to restore it to its former place of importance in the Sea Island economy. Faithful work, then, became synonymous with raising Sea

Picking cotton.

Island cotton, the major cash crop of the Sea Islands. Missionaries took every opportunity to encourage former slaves to work the crop. They used many persuasive tactics, ranging from Biblical teachings through sermons to threats of enslavement. None proved very effective. When the missionaries appealed to the Negro "drivers" (slaves who had control over field slaves) for help, former slaves responded by working the cotton. Drivers knew their people and the farm operation better than anyone else on the plantations. They were also accustomed to controlling other slaves. They spoke the same language and had the same experiences of slavery, so they were in a better position to appeal to the former slaves' loyalty to President Lincoln for emancipating them. They certainly wouldn't want President Lincoln to think they were too lazy to work.

Perhaps the greatest benefit of the Port Royal Experiment was the establishment of schools for ex-slaves. Formal education for freed slaves began on St. Helena Island, South Carolina, one year after the Civil War began and five months after the "gun shoot" at Bay Point. Laura Towne, a teacher, physician, and aboli-

Penn School, founded in 1862, first school for freed slaves in the United States.

tionist from Philadelphia, established Penn School in an old plantation house called the Oaks. She later sent for her friend, Ellen Murray. The two women began teaching the freed slaves of St. Helena Island in a makeshift classroom in April, 1862. They were joined in October of the same year by Charlotte Forten, the first African-American teacher at Penn School.

Charlotte Forten was a well-educated, free black woman from Philadelphia. Her grandfather, James Forten, owned a successful sail loft where he made sails for ships. He hired Caucasians and African Americans to work in his shop. As a member of a free black, well-to-do family, Charlotte was surrounded by many of the luxuries of life. She was also surrounded by many influential people in the antislavery movement. Her family entertained such dignitaries as abolitionists James Mott, Lucretia Mott, and William Lloyd Garrison. John Greenleaf Whittier, the famous poet from Boston, Massachusetts, was a frequent visitor in the Forten home and a personal friend of her family.

Despite her family's wealth and prominence, Charlotte was not allowed to attend the white schools in Philadelphia, a practice which was very offensive to her father, Robert Forten. To show his disapproval of the segregated system, Robert had his daughter taught at home by his sister, Margaretta Forten, who was a teacher at the Sarah Mapp Douglass School. Later, Charlotte was sent to Salem, Massachusetts, to live with Charles and Sarah Redmond, lecturers for the Massachusetts Anti-Slavery Society. She enrolled in the Higginson School and excelled in all her studies.

Charlotte graduated from the Salem Normal School, and, at age eighteen, was hired by the Salem school board to teach fourth grade students at Epes Grammar School. It was during this period that she became even more aware of the plight of all African Americans — free, fugitive, or slave. She read every issue of Garrison's *Liberator*, and attended many of the antislavery meetings.

 Charlotte was persuaded by John Greenleaf Whittier to apply to the Port Royal Commission to help the freed people of the South Carolina Sea Islands. Charlotte applied and was accepted. Out of the fifty accredited agents of the Port Royal Relief Association which were chosen, she was the only African American. Consequently, she felt a great burden to do her very best to make her race proud of her. As a teacher of freed slaves, she was aware of her responsibility to teach them more than reading and writing. She felt obligated to teach them to respect themselves and their race.

The three teachers from Philadelphia — Towne, Murray, and Forten — faced the formidable task of trying to keep Penn School going with limited funds, supplies, clothing, furniture, and medical supplies. St. Helena was occupied by Union forces so the residents were in no immediate danger of being caught up in battle. Occasionally, however, Confederate rebels would get on the island undetected. They killed people and cattle and burned Union storehouses where supplies were kept.

Charlotte expressed some concern for her safety at the Oaks, the plantation where she lived. Many nights she stayed awake wondering if the sounds she heard were those of Confederate rebels who had come to do her harm.

Laura Towne and her staff helped to bring stability into the lives of thousands of newly released slaves on St. Helena. The teacher-missionaries worked long hours and performed many different jobs. They were teachers, physicians, nurses, extension agents, and missionaries. Each of them taught as many as fifty-eight children during the day. At night, they taught the parents of their daytime students.

Charlotte wrote in her journal that "All teachers, in addition to their regular work, are encouraged to interest themselves in the moral, religious, and social improvement of the families of their pupils, to visit them in their homes; to instruct the women and girls in sewing and domestic economy; to encourage and take part in religious meetings and Sunday Schools."

By 1864, more than two thousand freedmen were being taught in the thirty schools scattered over the Sea Islands. Many schools began in churches with three and four classes going on in one room. They received supplies from benevolent societies like the Philadelphia Port Royal Relief Association. Teachers also received their instruction from the relief association.

Eager children walked as many as ten miles to get to Penn School. Charlotte Forten had never seen children so eager to learn. She said that they were as happy about coming to school as children in the North were when it was time to go outside to play. Older children who, during the summer, toiled in the fields from sun-up to about noon, came to school after work with the same enthusiasm. Ms. Forten and other teachers soon found that Negro children were just as capable as any other children of equal age and circumstance.

The Civil War ended in 1865, and a brief period of prosperity for the Sea

Rowing to Penn School, St. Helena Island, SC.

Islanders began. By the end of the war, some Negro farmers were making their second crop on what they called their "little plantations." Others who had chickens, fish, and vegetables to sell found a ready market for their goods among the soldiers and missionaries who stayed on when the war ended. Those freedmen who went to work in the army camp earned good wages. Youth who volunteered for the army were given a $300 bonus by the government. This was enough money to buy ten acres of land, and to have some left over for their personal use. The Freedmen's Bureau was still in place to help the needy.

Penn School had a tremendous influence on the quality of life on St. Helena Island where the largest number of freed slaves stayed after the war. On its sprawling campus, classes in agriculture, basketmaking, nursing, cobbling, canning, ironworks, and a host of other trades were taught to eager young people, some of whom rowed distances through marshes in rickety boats to get to Penn School. During this time also, dormitories were built so that students could live on campus.

During the early years of Reconstruction many former slaves purchased small parcels of land, bought carts, buggies, and horses and built cabins. But, the new prosperity was short-lived because it was based on a wartime economy. They soon found that they had to settle down to the economic reality of self-sufficiency if they were going to survive on the Sea Islands. Therefore, they began to raise larger "truck crops" which usually consisted of vegetables such as sweet potatoes, corn, and hominy and grits. They also raised chickens, pigs, and oxen for their own use.

African Americans experienced a brief period of leadership and success during Reconstruction. In Beaufort, South Carolina, a few freedmen purchased the homes of their former masters. Robert Smalls bought the Prince Street house of Henry McKee and ran a successful business on Bay Street. He also served in the South Carolina legislature from 1868 to 1875 and in the United States House of Representatives from 1875 to 1879 and again from 1882 to 1887.

Family farming, St. Helena Island, SC.

In 1870, phosphate was discovered in coastal South Carolina, providing work and pay for Negro laborers. Leaving their wives and children to work the farm, men went to work in the phosphate mines to make "cash money." When the phosphate beds were depleted, oyster factories were built, offering employment as hands in the factories or laborers on the oyster boats.

On the down side, Sea Island cotton crops barely brought in enough money to pay taxes on their land and to buy clothing. Negro farmers had to scrape up tax money, no matter what the sacrifice because they understood that their land was the basis of their security. Hard times such as these drove many young people from the islands. Young men and women, mostly in their teens, were sent off the islands to work as servants in the North or in Savannah and Charleston.

Regardless of the changes and challenges that resulted from the "gun shoot," it still marked the day that the first chains of slavery, no matter how tentative, were broken on the Sea Islands.

Four
SEEKING AND SHOUTING:
Gullah Religious Traditions

$\mathcal{I}$n the slave communities of the Sea Islands, two very different religious cultures merged to form a Creole religion, a mixture of African and European religious beliefs and practices. Sea Island slaves cleverly wrapped their African values and religious practices in a blanket of the acceptable European rituals practiced by their masters. They adopted those features of European religion that they liked and adapted them to suit the more familiar religious practices of their ancestors. Because Africans of the Sea Islands kept their strong attachment to their countries and were so isolated from other cultural groups, they maintained the mixture of Christianity and African religious practices much longer than elsewhere in the South. This blending of African and European religions created an energetic and positive mixture that is uniquely Gullah.

One of the religious traditions which survived well into the twentieth century was "seeking." Seeking combined the European practice of being instructed in the catechism, a book of questions and answers about the scriptures and Christianity, and the African initiation ceremonies in which the young were required to go into the bush to be instructed by the older members of their tribe.

Making the decision "to give your life to the Lord" was, and still is, taken very seriously among the Gullah. Giving your life to the Lord meant that you gave up all "worldly" activity and pleasures and concentrated on being a good Christian. In the Gullah churches, each person was required to go through the lengthy process of seeking before being accepted into the fellowship of a church. The Gullah practice of seeking one's soul's salvation was much more involved than in other African-American churches. The seeker in the Gullah church began his faith walk with a dream or vision. The seeker was matched with a "leader," a "spiritual teacher," or "spiritual mother," who guided the seeker through the seeking experience. Then he was required to remove himself from the rest of the world, including family and friends. He spent time alone in meditation and prayer, usually in the backyard or often in the woods at night. The seeker gave up everything while praying. Each evening the seeker told his dream to his spiritual leader who interpreted the dream or vision.

Carrie Bell Brown, a native of St. Helena Island, South Carolina, and Executive Director of the Dayton Christian Center in Dayton, Ohio, recalled, "You gave up play and fun time when you were 'praying.' You had to go out into the backyard, and, in some communities, literally into the woods where there were mosquitoes and other insects. It was your time apart to pray to God and ask for forgiveness."

Carrie Bell explained that "You 'came through your seeking' if in your dream, someone gave something to you." This type of dream was interpreted by the spiritual leader to be the gift of the Holy Spirit. "I told my spiritual teacher about someone giving me a card with a picture of Christ holding the lamb on one side and the 23rd Psalm on the other," she remembered.

When the spiritual teacher was confident that her charge had "come tru" [through], she called all of the elders of the church together to listen to the seeker's dream. If they were all satisfied that the seeker's experiences were genuine, the seeker was taught the catechism to understand his faith. The seeker was then quizzed on his knowledge of the catechism by the praise house committee and deacons of the church. If he passed, he became a candidate for baptism. If he failed, he went before a tribunal court, consisting of the leader and the committeemen.

The final step of the seeking process occurred when the "presider" or "ward" came to the local praise house to lead the worship. The presider or ward was like a Bishop; he was highly respected and revered. Everyone showed up at praise when the presider came. People from neighboring praise houses and churches packed the church. They came to celebrate. They sang hymns, spirituals, and lis-

Lining a hymn. Pictured is Carrie Bell Brown, St. Helena Island, SC.

tened to the presider deliver his sermonette. The period of seeking was long and involved and required prayer, fasting, and meditation.

The time between "seeking" (expressing a desire to seek one's soul's salvation) and actually "coming tru" (receiving approval of elders) could take months. A few seekers were lost in the lengthy process, but most made it through and believed, without a doubt, that they had come through and were changed.

The Gullah practice of seeking may seem foreign to many people. Others might be reminded of the "mourner's bench" ritual which was practiced in many African-American churches, especially in rural areas. The candidate for church membership came forward, usually during revival, and expressed his desire to accept the Lord. He was asked to sit on the front pew to show that he was "mourning" his sinful ways.

According to Carrie Bell Brown, the mourning bench in Gullah churches was located in the rear of the church.

"Those who were Christians sat on the benches in the front of the church, mainly the women and girls. The last bench in the church was called the mourner's bench. This was where the 'sinners' or 'ungodly' persons, those who had not 'prayed' and been baptized sat," Carrie Bell noted.

Seeking was just one of the traditions which survived in the Gullah churches

Worship in a plantation in South Carolina.

38

and praise houses. Another was the pomp and ceremony of baptisms. Gullah baptismal services continued to be colorful and joyous occasions well into the twentieth century. A number of contemporary Gullah people remember baptisms as festive times that lasted the whole day and a good part of the night. Gullah baptisms were frequently held at ebb (low) tide so that the sins of the converts would be taken out with the tide.

Charles Hunter, a former slave who lived on St. Simons Island, Georgia, said, "We hab tuh wait till a Sunday wen a ebb tide come at a good time, cuz it duh ebb tide wut carry yuh sin away."

Baptisms, at least on St. Helena Island, took place twice a year, in May and August. The preacher or leader led the processional of white-clad converts and church members from the praise house down to the banks of the nearby creek or river. As they walked along the dusty roads, the sounds of spirituals went airborne throughout the community. Songs such as "All Muh Sins Done Wash Away" told the story of being baptized at ebb tide. The preacher then took the candidates, one at a time, and dipped them in the creek. Then he prayed that the water would wash their sins away.

After baptism, there was a break to allow the deacons to set up communion. Then the congregation would come together again for the "right hand of fellowship" which welcomed the new members into the fellowship of that church. After this service, there was a period of singing and shouting.

Worship in the Gullah church followed a precise order of service, probably the influence of the Episcopal and Presbyterian churches. The lively meetings opened with a spiritual followed by a hymn which the worship leader "lined" (called out) two lines at a time. Often the songs of whites were improvised or changed by the praise leaders. After the hymn, the leader called for prayer. Another passage of scripture was read. It was followed by another prayer and testimony from the members. Finally, the scripture was read and interpreted by the leader.

The "shout" was usually the last part of the praise meeting, often lasting well into the night. The old-fashioned "ring shout" combined the African traditions of the circle and ring dance with Christian values. During the shout period,

Praise House at Eddings Point, St. Helena Island, SC.   *Inside Praise House at Eddings Point.*

benches were pushed back to the wall, leaving a large open space in the center of the room like a dance hall. From the very beginning, the Sea Islanders enjoyed the shout for they believed it "exercised the frame." In their opinion, the shout was good physical exercise for the body.

Laura Towne, founder of Penn School on St. Helena Island, thought the ring shout was offensive and primitive. Writing in her diary about the first time she witnessed a shout, she said, "Tonight I have been to a 'shout,' which seems to me certainly the remains of some idol worship. The negroes sing in a kind of chorus... three standing apart to lead and clap... then all the others go shuffling round in a circle following one another with not much regularity, turning round occasionally and bending the knees, and stamping so that the whole floor swings. I never saw anything so savage."

Shouts were performed as much for entertainment as worship. Charlotte Forten wrote about how children "performed" the shout to entertain the teachers and missionaries in the evenings.

"The children form a ring and move around in a kind of shuffling dance, singing all the time. Four or five stand aside and sing very energetically, clapping their hands, stamping their feet, and rocking their bodies to and fro. These children are the musicians to whose rhythm the shouters keep perfect time." Shout songs which were also called "running spirituals" usually accompanied the shout.

But we don't have to go back to 1862 for an account of the shout. Carrie Bell described it from a modern-day Gullah perspective. "Some of the steps of dances that people do today with the foot movements were shouting steps that they did at that [during her childhood] time. We would gather in a circle and chant a tune to a slow beat where we would move slowly in a 'rocking and swaying' motion. Then the rhythm would change and there would be clapping and singing and all kinds of foot and body movements."

Carrie Bell's only regret is that so few people on St. Helena Island celebrate with the shout anymore. "My eighty-six-year-old father is still a whiz at this," she related proudly.

While most of the old religious practices have disappeared, some are still being preserved in the older Gullah churches and praise houses. I was fortunate to be invited to worship at a church on Johns Island, South Carolina, where members continue to conduct worship in the old way, incorporating at least some of the African religious traditions of trances, spirit possession, and the shout.

Community Pentecostal Church, formerly Rising Star Lodge, is one of about five praise houses on the Sea Islands with an active Gullah congregation. It is nestled almost protectively between live oak trees and lush green vines. The little one-room, white church, which is surrounded on three sides by sleepy, live oak trees and a thick stand of jade and ivory honeysuckles, is a memorial to an age-old tradition of worship.

A few yards beyond this natural hedge is the local "hangout" where men gathered on this balmy April morning for fellowship of a different kind. While wandering around the church grounds, smelling the wonderful fragrance of the honeysuckle blossoms and plucking a few to taste the sweet nectar, my sister, my mother, and I tried with all our might to eavesdrop on the conversations coming through the "viny" barrier.

Community Pentecostal had no frills, and, in its simplicity, Sea Islanders came to worship in the tradition of their African ancestors. The wooden benches were nailed to the walls. They had no backs to them and were just wide enough to sit comfortably. The ladies of the church placed homemade pillows on the floor in front of our bench so that we would be comfortable when we knelt to pray. Windows were opened to let in a cross breeze, but it also let in flies and bees. As I looked in the ceiling, I saw where dirt dobbers, a type of bee, had built their nests, and were just waiting for the chance to go and come through the open windows.

Church service at Community reminded me of the old-time revival meetings I attended as a child in Cartersville, Virginia. We were always welcomed by a highly respected person of the church. In this same tradition, we were warmly welcomed by Janie Hunter, Mother of the Church. Mother of the Church is a position of honor given to the oldest woman in the church. Her welcome was followed by about an hour of testimony and praise.

Worship service at Community had a definite rhythm. It became more and more spirited with each song or shout or the laying on of hands for healing. Each testimony or prayer was punctuated by a song. Songs of faith and hope dominated the service, and everyone, even visitors, were encouraged to share. When my sister, Virginia, shared her struggle with cancer, the whole church went into a spiritual frenzy as though she were a close and personal friend. Special prayers

Community Pentecostal Church sign, Johns Island, SC.

Community Pentecostal Church, Johns Island, SC.

were prayed for her, and Elder Hunter "laid hands" on her for healing. It was a joyous time.

Songs which began slowly suddenly picked up tempo and became very fast before slowing down again. Janie Hunter's daughter Tina played the drums and led many of the songs. Musical instruments were really not necessary because the unique hand-clap of the Gullah worshipers served as instruments, keeping perfect rhythm to accompany the melodious voices.

Elder Hunter is the Pastor of the Community Pentecostal Church and son of Janie Hunter. His sermon about HOPE was delivered in traditional African-American fashion, plainly and feverently. True to the tradition, he evoked frequent responses from the congregation. The "Yes, Lords," "Amens," and "Hallelujahs" filled the small sanctuary. The more the congregation responded, the more spirited the sermon became. This part of the worship service was truly reminiscent of my home church.

Before long, worshipers were caught up in the "spirit" and began to shout. The shouts resembled the shouts explained earlier in the chapter, but they were somewhat less animated. We were surprised to see children shout too, but Janie Hunter explained that her family sets aside a time each Sunday evening to teach the children the songs and shouts of their ancestors.

Just before service ended, Elder Hunter came down from the pulpit and stood at the altar. He was still not convinced that everyone who needed some type of healing — whether physical, mental, or spiritual — had received it or had been released from the problem. So he extended a second invitation to come to the altar for intercessory prayer. While he was talking, a woman came forward. Elder Hunter talked with her for a moment and then he stretched out his hand to touch her. As soon as he touched her forehead, the woman fell backward in what appeared to be a trance. Her limp body was caught by two men who were standing behind her. I had never witnessed this display of faith.

When all of the elements of worship were put together, the shouts, the music, the laying on of hands, and the sermon, Community Pentecostal Church assumed a festive, yet reverent, air that took even my seventy-three-year-old mother back in time. In this enclave of Sea Island beauty, the small Pentecostal

Church remains a shrine to a century-old tradition of worshiping in the Gullah tradition which is likely to be practiced for centuries to come.

I experienced another type of worship when I visited Sam "Papa" Brown's home on St. Helena Island as guest of his daughter Carrie Bell. It was a family worship in song. Besides getting a good history lesson on worship in the Gullah praise house, I also learned metered hymns. Growing up, I had heard the elderly men and women of my church sing certain songs. They were sung slowly and had a very different beat. I learned from Carrie's family that night that these songs were metered hymns.

Carrie and her cousin Sadie Jenkins took turns lining the short meter and the long meter hymns from the hymnal. I was surprised to see a hymnal without any musical notes. In the Gullah hymnal, the words to the songs were printed with an explanation as to the type of metered hymns they were.

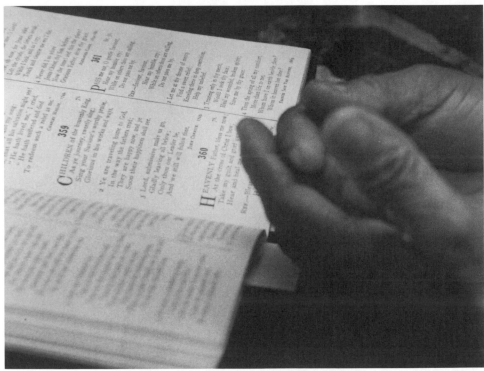

Lining a metered hymn, St. Helena Island, SC.

"Papa" Brown's voice is still strong and resonant.   *Sadie Jenkins, resident of St. Helena Island, SC.*

Gloria Wright, Carrie's cousin from Savannah, Georgia, proved that not everyone can line a hymn. Lining is a skill which takes a lot of practice. On the other hand, Sadie and Carrie lined with ease. Sadie lined first. "I was a wandering sheep. I did not love the fold. I did not love my shepherd's voice. I would not be controlled," she read confidently. Then she asked, "Would someone give us the tune of this song in short meter?"

Without hesitation, Papa's resonant, base voice rung out with amazing strength and clarity as he set the pattern for the rest of us to follow. We sang hymns and spirituals, clapped the calypso-style Gullah hand-clap, laughed, and rejoiced well into the night. Another Gullah worship experience had come to an end.

Five

DE HAG GONNA RIDE YOU:
Gullah Folklore

$\mathcal{G}$ullah folklore is like a thick pot of their unique Frogmore stew, a special stew made up of succulent shrimp, potatoes, corn on the cob, and hot sausage. The stew, which is still prepared by the residents of St. Helena Island, South Carolina, is named for a small area on the island called Frogmore. It is rich and tantalizing. Gullah folklore is also rich and tantalizing. It bubbles over with humor, originality, flavorful customs, superstitions, and intriguing characters. Gullah tales are heavily spiced with hags, haints, clever rabbits, flying people, witty slaves, and rolling snakes. Together, these characters make up the scrumptious Gullah tales that have been preserved by the keepers of culture and stories, the old griots and storytellers such as Janie Hunter who learned them from their African ancestors.

As in the West Indies and in Africa, rhymes, songs, and riddles are important to storytelling. Mrs. Janie Hunter begins her storytelling sessions with a song, followed by several riddles.

"How are ya'll?" Mrs. Hunter asked the sea of eager listeners who had been sitting all afternoon on hard, gray folding chairs under the mossed-draped live oak trees at Penn Center.

"Fine. Great. Okay," replied the chorus of voices.

"Wanna hear a story or song?" she asked.

Again, the mixed responses rose from the crowd, "Song. Story. Song. Story."

"Somebody wanna hear story. Somebody wanna hear song," she chuckled into the mike.

"What ya'll wanna hear?" she asked teasingly.

Singer/storyteller Janie Hunter, Johns Island, SC.

Before our words reached the stage, she broke into a song, "Oh…oh…no need to worry. Oh…oh…no need to worry. Oh…oh…no need to worry. Sun gonna shine in my door someday."

Mrs. Hunter instructed us to "put your hands together." This was our invitation to clap and sing along with her. We eagerly accepted, filling the afternoon air with our voices and our hands.

Mrs. Hunter made the transition from song to riddles without any warning. "Why does the chimney smoke?" she quizzed.

A mixture of wrong answers rang out from the audience.

"Give up?" she asked eagerly.

"Chimney smoke 'cause it can't chew," she laughed.

"One more riddle. Ya'll ready? When I leave home, I have two packs with me. One was a bag with a pretty little duck in it, and the other was a bag of money. Now, I wanna' give it away. Who want the money?" she asked. "Hold your hand up. Who want the duck? Hold your hand up." Janie Hunter pointed to the few people who raised their hands and threw her head back in laughter.

She continued the riddle. "The duck and the luck was swimming in the pond, the luck got drowned, but the duck keep on." Then she took time to explain the moral of the story. The money went straight to the bottom of the pond, but the duck was saved because it could swim.

As the oohs and aahs died down, Janie Hunter slid to the edge of the metal folding chair to begin her story. *"Once 'pon a time there were two children, Jack and Mary. Their parents were so poor, they couldn't buy Jack and Mary no present. But they save their nickels, dimes, and pennies until they save enough money to buy the children a present. They bought them three dogs, Barney McKay, Doodle-Dee-Do, and Sue-Boy. They bought Jack a bow and arrow. The children were so happy to get their present. Jack asked if he and Mary could go for a walk in the woods. Their parents said they could go. Now, Jack was a very wise boy. He went to the barn and got three grains of corn and put them in his pocket...."* A few minutes into the story, she had completely enchanted her listeners. In the tradition of her ancestors, she interspersed chants and moans throughout her rendition of two clever children who narrowly escaped being eaten by a "witchcraft" lady. The chants and wails moved the story along and they also allowed the audience to participate.

"Then Jack threw the last grain of corn, and it made the bridge bend, and that's the way the story end!" Mrs. Hunter ended her story amidst a thunderous applause from an appreciative audience.

The real delight of any Gullah story is in the telling. Gullah storytellers take their time. They savor each word. The rise or fall of the voice, the movement of the hands, a knowing chuckle, a riddle, a song, or a well-placed moment of silence are techniques used by the sable storytellers of the Sea Islands in much the same way as African storytellers.

Even though the African tales took on new life in the Sea Islands, the flavor, especially in the telling of the tales, has been maintained. Characters changed to fit the physical environment of the new country and the circumstances of slavery. Trickster Hare became the clever Brer Rabbit, and the mischievous slave named John outwitted his master any time he felt like it. Both characters played the role of trickster, making it their life's work to outwit and gain victory over animals or persons stronger or more powerful than themselves. Therefore, the basic idea of the weak outsmarting the strong found in most African stories remained in all the Gullah stories.

The Gullah folktales so familiar to most of us are the Brer Rabbit tales, featuring the cunning rabbit as the hero. In most of these tales, trickster Rabbit is in some kind of mental competition with an animal or person who is larger or stronger than himself. Brer Rabbit rarely ever does any physical work. Instead he tries to use his wit and cunning to get what he wants. The Gullah people also tried, through their stories, to explain various phenomenon in nature. The story that follows is just one of many how and why stories.

"De Reason Brer Rabbit Wears a Short Tail"

One evening Brer Wolf asked Brer Rabbit if he wanted to go fishing with him the next day. Brer Rabbit agreed to go. But next morning, when Wolf went to Brer Rabbit's house to get him like he promised, Brer Rabbit told him that he didn't want to go fishing because he had plenty of "bittle" [food] in his home.

So Brer Wolf went fishing by himself. When Brer Wolf left, Brer Rabbit followed him. Well, in the evening 'round about sundown, Wolf had caught a tub full of fish and he started for home. Brer Rabbit hide in the bushes to wait for him. When the Wolf came long the path, Brer Rabbit ran out and fell down in the path like he was dead. When Wolf saw him, he stopped and looked!

Wolf said, "Hi! How is this? Brer Rabbit is dead? This is a very strange thing. I left him well this morning. This will be very hard for his family."

Wolf took off down the path to notify Brer Rabbit's family, taking his tub of fish with him. As soon as he was gone, Brer Rabbit jumped up and ran through the bushes until he was ahead of Brer Wolf. Then he fell down in the path just like he did before.

When Brer Wolf had gone about a mile farther on he met him. Then he stopped and said, "Eh! Eh! so many dead Brer Rabbits today. What can this mean? Didn't I just pass one dead Brer Rabbit back yonder? And now here is another one stretched out in the path. Maybe I can go back and fetch him, if I hurry."

So he went back down the path to fetch the dead Brer Rabbit, leaving his tub of fish behind this time. As soon as he was out of sight, Brer Rabbit jumped up and ran off with Wolf's tub of fish.

When Wolf reached the place where he saw the first Brer Rabbit and found him gone, he was astonished! He search the bushes on both sides of the road — searched them good, but he couldn't find so much as a hair. Puzzled, Brer Wolf went back to the place where he left his tub of fish. And his fish were all gone! Well, Brer Wolf was worried. He didn't know what to think. So he decided to go to Brer Rabbit's house. And there he heard a great noise. Scrape, scrape!—Brer Rabbit and wife and children— the whole family was cleaning fish.

The door was fastened. And when Wolf knocked, no one answered the door.

When he saw that Rabbit and them were not going to answer, Wolf stood back and hollered, "Never mind, Brer Rabbit, you ol' rascal, I'll fix you this night." Brer Wolf went home and got a hatchet and plenty of black pepper. By the time he got back, Brer Rabbit and his family had cooked his fish and ate their supper. Now they were sitting around the fire.

Well, Wolf built a big fire right close to the Rabbit's door so that the wind would carry the smoke through all the cracks in the house. Then he threw lots of black pepper in the fire to strangle Brer Rabbit and his family.

Brer Rabbit, his wife, and all the children climbed up in the loft to get out of the way of the smoke. Then Wolf found a little crack in the chimney, and he threw black pepper in there, too. Finally, the whole house and the loft was full of peppery smoke.

When Rabbit and them couldn't stand the smoke any longer, they climbed out on the roof of the house. They were afraid to go down because they knew Wolf would keep his promise. Wolf was down below laughing.

Wolf said, "The first one to fall down here I'm going to kill him with my hatchet."

And all the time he was throwing black pepper in the fire.

Well, that peppery smoke got very bad. Brer Rabbit and his family coughed and coughed until they got weak. Wolf knew that they couldn't stand it much longer. One by one, all of the rabbits except Brer Rabbit himself were overcome by the smoke and fell to the ground. Brer Wolf looked up at Brer Rabbit, coughing and hanging on the roof.

He laughed and said, "Ah, ha! ol' fellow, you're hanging on still, huh? You've done well, but I have to get you."

Well, Rabbit hung on as long as he could. The smoke choked him and the cough strangled him until he almost fell. At last he saw that he had to go too. So he put one hand in his pocket and filled up his mouth with tobacco. He chewed it until his mouth was full of tobacco juice. Then he let go! Wolf looked up to see Rabbit fall.

Brer Rabbit spit out the whole mouthful of tobacco juice right in Wolf's eye, and blinded him. Wolf couldn't do anything but strike after Rabbit with his hatchet. He cut off his tail. So since then you always see Brer Rabbit and his children with short tails.

Next in importance and favor to the animal tales are the stories about John, the resourceful and ingenious slave. Like Brer Rabbit, John was not fond of hard work. He seized every opportunity to find ways to avoid it too. It was a lot more fun to get what he wanted from Massa without exerting himself. Even after the Civil War, when John was no longer a slave, he continued to show his superior cunning over his former boss.

"Tops and Bottoms"

John had always dreamed of farming his own piece of land, but he didn't own any. After the Civil War, he stayed on the plantation where he had grown up. John noticed that Old Boss had not cultivated a large area of rich bottomland for two years. John began to think about ways to trick Old Boss into letting him farm that piece of land. It was just sitting there doing nothing, he thought.

So John went to his boss and asked him if he could farm the bottomland.

"That's the best piece of land I own," said his greedy boss. "I've been meaning to plant cotton on it, but I've been so busy I just hadn't gotten around to it," he lied.

"Yes, Sir," John answered politely.

"But, I guess I could rent it to you and we can go halves on the crop. You get half and I'll get half," he continued.

"That's fine with me, Boss. Just fine," John agreed. "But what half do you want?"

Bewildered by John's question, Boss scratched his head. "What do you mean what half? I want half of the crop, that's all," he answered emphatically.

"I understand that, Boss, but I still want to know which half? Do you want the top half or the bottom half?" John persisted.

Thinking that John was talking about planting cotton, he answered, "I'll take the top half."

"Okay, Boss. That's a deal."

John could hardly wait for the ground to thaw from winter. He plowed the bottomland and got it ready for planting. By early June, the bottomland was a sea of green as the sweet potato vines covered the land.

John went up to the Big House to ask Old Boss to come look at their fine *crop. Boss knew it was early for cotton to be harvested, but he went with John anyway. When he saw the land covered with green vines, he almost fainted.*

"Ain't this one beautiful crop?" John asked proudly. "Now, what do you want to do with your tops, Boss?" he asked.

Boss's mouth fell open in dismay, and he walked away in a huff. As soon as he cooled down, he began to scheme against John for the next crop.

Again, before the ground thawed, John went to Boss to ask him if he could rent the land.

"You planning to do tops and bottoms again, John?" Old Boss asked knowingly.

"That's right, Boss. If it's okay with you, of course."

"Oh, sure, John. It's fine with me, but this year I'll take bottoms and you take tops. Just make sure you bring in a good crop like you did last year," he ordered.

At harvest time, John invited Old Boss to take a look at their fine crop.

"We did it again this year, Boss," John exclaimed. "I believe I'll probably get fifty bushels of wheat an acre," he crowed. "What do you want to do with all your straw?"

Boss was too angry and ashamed to answer. He stormed off across the field in a real fury, determined to pay John back next time. Old Boss spent the whole winter thinking of a way to outwit John. He felt sure he had come up with a fool-proof plan. Just like clockwork, John was back in early spring to get permission to farm the bottomland.

"Which half you want this year, Boss?" asked John.

"Listen, you fooled me twice, but you can't fool me a third time. This year, I'm taking the tops and the bottoms," Boss answered.

"Tops and bottoms?" John asked. "Tops and bottoms, Boss?" John repeated. "What do I get?"

"You get the middle, John. Now you can take it or leave it."

"Guess I don't have much choice, Boss," said John.

Old Boss had the best spring and summer he had had in a long time, for he knew John couldn't come up with a crop that had a middle. When John came to get Old Boss to look at their crop, he went happily. But his eyes nearly popped out of his head when he saw row after row of tall cornstalks covering the whole field.

John chuckled, "You got yourself quite a heap of tassels and stalks, Boss. What're you planning to do with them?"

This was the last straw! Old Boss took out across the field, waving his hands in the air and mumbling to himself like he had lost his mind.

Hags and haints also hold a respectable place in Gullah folklore. Although these stories are not told as regularly as they were in the late nineteenth and early twentieth centuries, they are still important to note. Folklorists, who interviewed former slaves during this period, found that they talked about hags and haints very willingly, many of them relating real-life encounters with the skin-shedding hags and frightful haints. The stories came complete with advice on how to get rid of the wretched "spirits" or ways to appease them so they wouldn't bother you anymore.

Most folks believe that hags are witches who live normal lives during the day. But, at night they shed their skin and go out to "ride" folks in their sleep. It is a common belief that hags spend their nights "riding" people. This means that they sit on the chest of their victims and make them have nightmares. Some say that they suck up the victim's voice so that she can't scream or call out to anyone.

A few people claim to have actually touched a hag. You may not be able to see them, but you can certainly feel them, they allege. Those who have touched a hag describe the sensation as "touching warm raw meat." When punched, they say she has the elastic quality of rubber.

Stories of the skin-shedding hags probably have their beginnings in the West Indies where the people believe that hags or witches shed their skins after midnight and travel around at will. Another carryover from the West Indies is that the hag is part witch and part vampire. She can fly and she can suck blood.

"Dey goes in en sucks your blood troo yer nose," said one old man.

Hags especially like to ride very young children and old people. One old woman complained of being exhausted from having been ridden by the hag for seven years. One night she decided that she had had enough. The old woman put lots of wood on her fire so that it would give light throughout the night. Before going to bed, she placed a sifter over the keyhole in her door because she heard that hags are curious and superstitious and that they will stop to investigate anything different. When the hag got in the keyhole (that's how they usually enter the house) she was surprised to see the sifter. The curious hag stopped to count the holes in the sifter. It took her all night because she kept losing her count and had to start over again. So the hag spent the night in the sifter instead of riding the old woman. For the first night in seven years, the old lady got a full night's sleep. From that night on, the old woman placed the sifter over the door to keep the hag out.

Janie Moore said that "A hag won't cross your doorsill if you put a broom across it." This is very much in keeping with the hag's reputation of being curious and superstitious. Some say that the hag will not only try to count the straws in the broom, but she will also try to measure the length of each one. Therefore, a broom might keep the old hag too busy to notice that the sun is coming up, and she'll get caught. Hags can't stand sunlight or salt so they always leave the victim's house before the sun rises and return to their bodies.

Like any folktale, there are many, many variations of the same story. The slip-skin hag stories vary a little with each teller. One version goes like this: *Once there was a young girl who was sent to Charleston to live with an old lady who was a hag. The hag was married. One night while the old woman and her husband were sleeping, the old woman got up. Her husband, who wondered where she went every night after midnight, decided to watch her leave. He saw her slip out of her skin and put it behind the door. As soon as she left, he got out of bed and got the salt. He found her skin and salted it just like he did when he salted hog meat. Just before dayclean, he saw the hag in the moonlight. She was coming through the crack in the door, looking raw.*

The old hag came up to the skin and whispered three time, "Skin, you no know me?" Then she started to slip back in her skin, but the salt stung so badly that she ran behind the door.

The next morning, the man called all the people in town to see the hag. When they saw her, they put her in a pan and burned her, because they knew that was the only way to get rid of the worrisome hag.

Haunts or "hants" as the Gullah call them are more powerful than hags. As spirits of the dead they can walk right through barred doors and walls. They are most likely to be seen when the moon is full, and they make strange things happen in the house like lifting the lid of a jar or causing a rocking chair to rock without anyone sitting in it. They'll do anything to scare the occupant of the house.

"I sho' does b'lieve in ha'nts 'cause I done heard one and I seed it too, lease-wise I seed its light," confessed a former slave.

Haints are everywhere, but they seem to prefer graveyards and swamps. Like hags, certain things must be done to ward off haints. Former newspaper columnist Francis Bradley gave this personal account. One day he happened upon an old pine log that he thought would be perfect for "lightwood" (used to start fires). He wanted to cut the wood up to take home with him. He asked his Gullah friend, Cephus, to help him put the lightwood in his car and offered to pay him by giving him most of the wood. Cephus agreed to help under the condition that he be allowed to put the wood on top of his woodpile until the "sun-hot" could run off the "swamp haints." According to Cephas, there were deep swamp haints which lived in the densest part of the swamp.

"Twernt no mebbe so with him 'bout dese haints," Cephas assured Francis Bradley. *"I knows what I'm talking 'bout. When I was nothin' but a lad of a boy, I used to hunt possums with my old grandpaw. Now that was a man that knowed his business. He larn't me 'bout all there was to know about swamp haints—showed 'em to me."*

Cephas declared that it takes at least a month of hot summer sun to get rid of the swamp haints. You must have a full moon with bright nights for the light swamp hants to find their way back home, and likewise a season of dark nights for the dark night haints to travel. After that time, it would be safe to put the wood in the house. He warned that if Francis were to put the wood in the house immediately, the haints would come in with the wood and bring all sorts of worry and bad luck.

Cemetery lore is also popular. "Dividing Souls" is one of the most well-liked stories about graveyards.

"Dividing Souls"

Two men who had stolen three bags of sweet potatoes carried them to the graveyard at the Baptist church to divide them equally between themselves. Well, just as they were getting started, a colored man walked by. The man heard strange noises, the thud, thud, thud of potatoes being thrown on each man's pile. Then he heard voices. Even though he was afraid, he stopped to listen.

"Dis one you'n [yours], dis dere mine."

The inquisitive traveler couldn't believe what he was hearing. The Lord and the Devil were dividing souls in the graveyard. He had to tell someone so he ran down the road until he met a white man.

"Say, Boss, the Devil and the Lord sharing souls in the graveyard over yonder," he panted. "If you don't believe me, come on, let's go back."

The two men started down the road toward the graveyard and stood by the gate to listen.

"Dis one you'n [yours], dis dere mine," said the thieves.

"Well, suh, if this don't beat all I ever seen," said the white man.

The two men stood at the gate listening for quite a while, spellbound by what they were witnessing.

When the thieves had finished dividing the potatoes in the bag, one of them remembered that in their haste to get in, they had dropped two of the sweet potatoes by the gate.

"What about the two at the gate?" asked one of the thieves.

Down the road the two men ran, almost ran themselves to death.

There are a few Gullah stories that resemble ones from other cultures. "Little Gal an Woof," told in the Gullah language, sounds very similar to "Little Red Riding Hood" and the "Gunniwolf."

Once 'pon a time was lil gal. Lil gal walkin' in woods. Lil gal see some flowah. Lil gal bruk de flowah-bruk de flowah and come on! Lil gal see a woof.

Woof seh, "Lil gal, sin a song for me lessn I eat you up!"

Lil gal sing, "Ta! Ta! Ta! Ta!"

Lil gal git way down de road. Woof meet lil gal agin.

Woof seh, "Sing dat song agin lessn I eat you up!"

Lil gal meet dat woof tree time. Lil gal sing dat song tree time. Lil gal git home tell huh muddah 'bout she hab tuh sing dat "Ta! Ta! Ta! Ta!" song for de woof lessn he eat de lil gal up.

Sep on de tin!

Tinny wouldn't bin!

Dat de way

My story end!

Reciting a rhyme such as this at the end of the story is very common among Gullah storytellers, especially if the storyteller knows something is lacking. This is another carryover from the West Indies.

Gullah storytellers have always kept their stories clean, refusing to tell anything obscene even to the folklorists who were collecting their stories. Gullah men would refuse to tell the part of the story which they called "man tales," opting instead to leave out large chunks of the story.

"I leave it der" was the usual response and no amount of coaxing could get them to go any further.

Holidays, Saturday night parties, and family gatherings still provide the occasions for storytelling and singing in the closely knit Gullah communities, but an outsider is not likely to hear these stories except through professional tellers.

Death, burial, and mourning make up a large part of Gullah folklore too. It is important to the people how and where their loved ones are buried. A few Gullah people still practice the West African custom of putting objects used by the deceased person on his or her grave. An assortment of eating utensils, medicine bottles, washbasins, and water jugs can still be found on graves in Gullah cemeteries.

I visited Daufuskie Island, a remote island off the coast of Hilton Head, a while back. Curious as to whether they still honored the tradition of putting objects on graves, I asked Yvonne Wilson, a native islander, about it.

"Not everyone believes in it, but I do. When I lost my baby, I put diapers, a pacifier, and his bottles with him," Yvonne explained.

The tradition of placing familiar objects on the graves has been traced back to the Congo (Angola) and other West African countries from which a large number of slaves came. This ritual was performed, among other things, to keep the spirit of the dead satisfied. Often the deceased got the very best object in the house. A new clock, a piece of china — the best that the family had to offer — was left at the grave to appease the spirit of the dead loved one.

If a mean-spirited person was being buried, no one wanted his spirit to be left behind. Therefore, mourners would form a tight circle around the grave until the casket was well covered with dirt.

If a mother died and left a young child, the child was passed over the grave so that the mother's spirit would not come back and take the baby away. Some say that the baby (child) had to be passed across the coffin before it left the house, others say the child had to be passed across the coffin at the gravesite.

"Dead moder will hant de baby, worry him in his sleep. Dat's de reason, when moder die, dy wil han' a little baby 'cross de box [coffin]," a Gullah woman explained to folklorist Elsie Clewes Parsons.

Other superstitions include not sweeping dust out of the house until the body goes out, and placing the last cup and saucer used by the deceased on his grave to keep him from fretting. Another practice is that of placing medicine bottles on the grave. If any medicine is left in the bottle, the bottle is turned upside down so that the medicine will soak into the grave. Glass objects should be covered up and turned toward the wall. Clocks are stopped at the time of death. Superstitions are plentiful in the Gullah culture. A few of the more familiar ones are listed.

Yvonne Wilson, resident/activist, Daufuskie Island, SC.

It is bad luck to sweep after sundown because you'll sweep yourself out of a home. This superstition may also be based on the African belief that the good spirits come into the house at night and may be swept out by mistake along with the dust.

When you hear a screech owl, it's a sure sign of death.

If a dog howls outside, it's a sign that somebody is dead or dying.

Never throw your hair outside because it is a part of your personal body and someone could use it to put a "fix" on you.

If bubbles form on top of your coffee, you will get money soon.

Rheumatism can be cured by carrying an Irish (white) potato in your pocket.

As long as there are people like Janie Hunter, Sam "Papa" Brown, Ronald and Natalie Daise, Frankie and Doug Quimby, the Hallelujah Singers, and other Gullah storytellers, the stories will never fade away entirely. For it is through these sages that they are kept and perpetuated in families, in communities, and in the country.

Six
DE GULLAH SPEAKS

*I*magine being bound for months to someone who speaks an entirely different language from yourself. Imagine also that once you arrive in the strange country, you see other Africans like yourself, but you don't all speak the same language. Or imagine that the person to whom you belong (your owner) speaks yet another language. Somehow, you must find a way to communicate with the other persons. What would you do? You'd probably find whatever similarities you could in the languages and use them to communicate, wouldn't you? That is exactly what the African slaves who were brought to the Sea Islands of South Carolina and Georgia did. They found similarities in the many African languages they spoke, and mixed them with the English language to form what is called a Creole "Gullah or Geeche" language.

A Creole language is a mixture of two or more languages that serves as the native language of its speakers, and aids in communication among people who have no common language. African slaves came from many parts of West Africa and spoke many different languages. Having the need to communicate among themselves, and learn "standard English" to communicate with their masters, they developed the Gullah language.

For years, white linguists (persons who study languages) referred to the Gullah or Geechee language as a dialect or a "corruption" of standard English. They studied the Gullah "dialect" in depth to dispute its African roots, and disputed the survival of African words in the Gullah language by linking frequently used words and phrases back to Europe. Another theory which they held was that slaves mimicked the "baby talk" that their masters used to communicate

62

with them. Finally, they believed that the African languages could not possibly have survived the long years of slavery.

Then along came the brash and brilliant Lorenzo Turner. As a highly educated African-American scholar and linguist, Turner challenged all of those theories held by white linguists. He prepared himself for the challenge. He became the first African-American member of the highly regarded Linguistic Society of America. He worked on American dialects for the *Linguistic Atlas* project, he published articles on the subject, and he went to England to study African languages. His greatest accomplishment was the publication of his book, *Africanisms in the Gullah Dialect*. This book, which was published in 1949, convinced other linguists that Gullah did indeed have its roots in Africa.

According to Turner, the most noted similarities in Gullah and the languages spoken in West Africa include the use of nouns, pronouns, verbs, and tense. Almost all Gullah nouns are singular, and in the Ibo language the singular form of a noun is the same as the plural. No distinction is made between the singular and plural of a verb in Gullah either. This practice is also common in the African languages. Finally, little importance is placed on the actual time when something took place. Therefore, the form of the verb used to refer to the present is also used to refer to the past.

African and African-American linguists like Lorenzo Turner have found numerous instances of African survivals in the Gullah language. They have traced the Gullah vocabulary back to African countries such as Senegal, Gambia, Sierra Leone, Ghana, Nigeria, and Angola where languages such as Wolof, Vai, Twi, Ewe, Yoruba, Mandinka, Ibo, Kongo are spoken.

A few Gullah words with African origins are listed and defined. As often as possible, I have given the language and/or country of origin. Most are taken from Turner's *Africanisms in the Gullah Dialect* and E. Mason Crum's *Gullah*.

A'min - Amen (Wolof)

be - to cultivate, to clean, to remove debris (Temme)

bid', bidi - small bird, small chicken (Kongo)

buckra - white man (Ibidio)

da (dada) - mother, nurse, or elder woman (Ewe)

dash away - to get rid of a bad habit

dayclean - dawn

de - to be (Igbo)

differ - a quarrel

e - pronoun for he, she, it

eh - yes (Igbo)

fanner - a large shallow basket made of wild grass and palmetto, used to
    thresh rice from its hull.

hudu - to cause bad luck to someone (Via)

kuta - tortoise, turtle (Mende)

nyam, nam - to eat

nanse - spider (Temme)

nana - elderly woman, grandmother (Twi)

oona, hoona - you, singular or plural, from the word "ona," meaning one or
    a single person

plat-eye - a prowling ghost or evil spirit

shut mout' - secretive or withdrawn

tata - father (Kongo)

tote - to pick up (Kongo)

toti frog - frog (Via)

uni - you, your (Ibo)

yam - sweet potato (Mende)

An interesting relationship between Gullah and the languages of West Africa is the use of the proverb to advise or instruct. African and Gullah proverbs use metaphors to relate real-life situations. "Take no more on your heels than you can kick off with your toes," "Every grin teeth don't mean laugh," "Every shut eye don't mean sleep," "Feed you with the corn and choke you with the cob," "Day is just an arm long, you can reach clean across it," "Don't fly so high dat you lit on a candle," and "Fire don't crack a full pot."

The Gullah language has gone through many phases. The seed of the language was planted in the "castles" and "forts" which held captive Africans awaiting transport to the Americas. It took root in the Sea Islands as their need to communicate became even greater. It reached its peak in usage during the eighteenth and nineteenth centuries when almost all Sea Island slaves spoke it. Use of the language declined from the early 1950s (when bridges were built connecting the islands to other islands and the mainland in the late 1970s) because of the negative stigmas attached to its speakers by outsiders.

Attitudes about the Gullah language were slow to change. Even in the African-American communities, persons who spoke Gullah were considered backward. The feeling was that if you wanted to get ahead in the world, you had to speak "standard" English. The Gullah persons to whom I spoke said they were made to feel bad for speaking their language.

"We were perceived as being 'backward' and called Geechies, a reference made to people who ate rice and talked bad! I spent a lot of energy trying to improve my speech, even though mine [speech] was not as strong as other islanders. Yet, the Gullah dialect is easily picked up by those who are not used to the speech pattern. At times, I am asked if I am from the West Indies," Carrie Bell remembers painfully. Janie Moore agrees. She, too, was made to feel inferior for the way she spoke. Even her teachers discouraged her from speaking her language.

The lyrical, West Indian flavor of the Gullah language is difficult to disguise though. Even the Gullah people who have learned "standard English" and speak in a so-called "refined" and proper way, have a difficult time disguising their accents. Two young successful business people who have lived in the Washington, DC, and Maryland area spoke at the Gullah Heritage Society's meeting about growing up on Johns Islands. Although they have been away from Johns Island and from speaking the language on a daily basis, I could detect the unique "clip" in their speech. One of the things they agreed on was how quickly they reverted to their language (Gullah) when they go home.

In most instances it took getting away from the Sea Islands for the natives to appreciate their language, particularly the African influence on their language. Carrie Belle Brown's awakening came in Brooklyn, New York, while involved in a ministry there. She met a lot of people from the Sea Islands who spoke as she did. But her interest was really aroused when she heard one of her professors speak about the Gullah language on the "Barry Farber Show." He told of the history of how the Gullah language evolved. He related how slaves were brought from West Africa and the West Indies and planted on the Sea Islands. He said that because the islands were so isolated, the speech patterns did not get assimilated into the speech patterns of the slave masters or other slaves elsewhere in the South.

Janie Moore's awakening to the African influence upon her language came when she went away to college and connected with Africans whose speech and customs were similar to her own. For the first time, she didn't feel backward.

Reverend Ervin Greene, Pastor of Brick Church on St. Helena Island and one of the volunteer translators of the Bible into Gullah, gained an appreciation of Gullah during the Caribbean Summer Institute of Linguistics in Jamaica in 1985.

In an interview with Ron Chepesiuk, Reverend Greene told the story of his conversation with a Jamaican cab driver. The cab driver spoke so much like the people in Beaufort County, South Carolina, that Reverend Greene had to tell him so.

The cab driver responded, "Yeah, mon. We come from the same home, but we just got off at different ports."

"That did it!" Reverend Greene exclaimed, finally realizing the importance of his language.

Seven
WITH THESE HANDS

$\mathcal{G}$ullah hands weave baskets, sew quilts, forge wrought iron, paint pictures, and make music in the tradition of their African ancestors. For centuries their hands have co-existed in the dual worlds of laborer and artisan. Thus, hands that picked cotton during the day, duplicated the exquisite quilt and coverlet patterns of their mistresses at night. Hands that hammered iron into horseshoes were just as capable of designing and forging intricate wrought iron gates. Hands that kept unwanted grass from choking out tender rice plants, pulled sweetgrass and wove it into the now famous coiled baskets.

Many African crafts and art forms were lost or hampered by slavery as slave craftsmen conformed to the tastes and wishes of their European masters. However, the African influence on the craftsmanship of the Gullah can be readily seen in the small, personal items they made for themselves. These items followed the shapes, materials, and techniques of those used in Africa. They included household and agricultural objects such as rice scoops, hoes, rakes, weaving shuttles, rice fanners (baskets), and clothing. They also include small decorative wooden objects such as pipes, canes, and musical instruments made for fun or gifts.

The most ancient and traceable African craft which has been preserved by the Gullah is basketmaking or basketsewing. Mary Twining, Sea Island resident and author, in establishing the connection between the African and Gullah techniques of making baskets, wrote, "Coiled basketry, one of man's oldest patterns, is easy to find in many societies. In the Sea Islands and the Senegambian region [Africa], however, we are dealing with groups whose genetic, historic, and linguistic links are known, so the basketry merely adds one more piece of evidence

"With these hands." Basketmaker in Charleston, SC, starting a basket.

that the same routes that carried the people and their language also transmitted the basketry patterns."

Mary Twining has done extensive research in the field of African retention in the Gullah culture. She spent a lot of time in West Africa and in the Sea Island region, researching clues and finding links between the two cultures. One of the things that is very clear to her is the similarities in the process in "sewing" the coiled baskets in both cultures. The process begins with sweetgrass being tied in an overhead knot. This knot forms the center of the base around which the basket is built. The basket is then sewn, one layer at a time, and stitched with palmetto leaves. Color is added by sewing in the russet-colored pine needles at intervals through the sewing process.

Route 17 which snakes its way along the South Carolina coast from just south of Myrtle Beach to Mt. Pleasant is peppered with gray, weather-worn stands where Gullah hands practice and display their art. A variety of decorative baskets, made in the African tradition, is proudly and aesthetically displayed on rough-hewn boards that make up the backs and sides of the stands. These road-

Basket stands along Route 17, Mt. Pleasant, SC.

side stands, though dulled by weather and sun, have become open-air museums where people can admire the handiwork of the Gullah basketmakers.

There are conflicting reports as to how the idea of marketing the baskets along Route 17 originated, but most agree that it began with a women who worked for the Works Projects Administration after World War I. This lady encouraged the Sea Islanders to revive the art of basketmaking that she believed was quickly vanishing from the culture. Seeing a ready market for the baskets along the heavily traveled Route 17, she convinced the Gullah ladies to make baskets for sale. She encouraged them to build individual stands to display and sell their creations. The idea caught on. Before long, the older woman were teaching the young girls and women how to sew the baskets in the tradition of their forebears.

Since then, basketmaking has been a profitable family business, especially in the Mt. Pleasant area. Families work together in the basketmaking business. Men and boys gather the rush, sweetgrass, palmetto, and the long pine needles which grow abundantly in the Low Country. The women make and sell the baskets. They sew the bulrush, sweetgrass, and pine needles into work and decorative baskets as well as decorative wall hangings, planters, door decorations, vases, and pocketbooks. No two pieces are the same. Men used to make baskets also. It is very interesting to note how the roles changed over the years since men were the first to teach basketmaking at Penn School. Making the coiled baskets was initially a man's job as it was with their African ancestors. Men sewed the strong "fanner" baskets, a flat basket with a small slanting rim used to separate the chaff from the rice. They made these baskets out of river rushes and white oak strips. Men also made decorative items like sewing baskets out of the finer grass, sewn with palmetto or oak strips. There are a number of ex-slave accounts of men basketweavers.

"Right after freedom, my father plaited baskets and mats. He shucked mops, put handles on rakes, and he did things like that in addition to his farming. He was a blacksmith at the time too. He used to plait collars for mules," recounted one former slave.

Now, however, one rarely sees a man "sewing." I understand that a few men still make baskets but they do it in the privacy of their homes. Women took over the craft because men migrated to cities and towns to find work on military bases, in factories, and hospitals to earn better incomes. As young children, boys and girls are both taught the skill of sewing baskets in basketmaking families, but boys tend to "put the baskets down" as teenagers because it's not considered man's work.

Basketsewers have learned the value of their art, and they are offended by people who want "something for nothing," as one Gullah basketsewer remarked to me.

The value of the sweetgrass baskets has gone up due, in large part, to the increased difficulty in getting to the much needed sweetgrass. Marshes and woodland that were once open to the harvesting of these materials for basketry are today off limits. Construction of residential areas, shopping centers, and private resorts have replaced the marshes and open fields. As a result, many basketmakers are having to import sweetgrass from other places like Savannah. Limited access to raw materials and the tremendous amount of skill and time it takes to

Basketmaker's stand, Old City Market, Charleston, SC.

sew the baskets have forced basketmakers to increase their prices in recent years.

Stories abound about tourists who stop to admire the baskets and complain about their prices. I witnessed one conversation at City Market in Charleston. A tourist stopped to look at the baskets. She picked up several large baskets and turned them over to price them. All the while, the basketmaker sat watching. Finally, the lady grumbled, "These are so expensive."

The basketweaver left her weaving and approached the customer. In her rich Gullah accent she scolded, "Miss, you must not know how much skill and time go into making my baskets. I cannot give them away."

The customer quickly put the basket down while the basketmaker continued to fume about "cheapskate."

In Mt. Pleasant I witnessed for myself what I had read about the roadside stands. Sure enough, the basket artists act as salespersons, historians, and guides. Although basketmakers are seldom chatty with strangers, they will give you details about their baskets. They tell you that each basket is different in some way and that each one has a unique story. Some shopowners allow you to wander around the stands while they continue to sew, others give guided tours of the merchandise. They tell you that each family has its own signature on its basket, something just a little different which distinguishes each family's baskets from another's. They are just as quick to tell you to be on the lookout for "shoddy" workmanship because it is a reflection on their craft.

The old City Market in historic Charleston is another busy market for the basketmakers. At one time, it was the primary market for them. It was zoned into

Basket vendors, Charleston, SC.

speciality market places: a beef market; three buildings for fruits, vegetables, grains, flowers, herbs, and kindling wood; a market for small meats; and a market for fish.

In 1939, the Charleston *Evening Post* published photographs of African-American merchants in fresh produce stalls, displaying a variety of products, including the popular woven baskets. Their stalls were located in the last two buildings near East Bay Street.

The sidewalks of Charleston have served as secondary outlets since the 1930s when peddlers brought kindling wood, flowers, and eggs to sell. These itinerant salespersons displayed their products in large, flat fanner baskets which they carried on their heads. Sometimes they held baskets on their arms as well.

The more well-established basketmakers have their shops inside City Market, a series of four long, open-ended, brick buildings built by slaves. These buildings are cut off by narrow side streets. It is at the entrances of this string of buildings that the majority of basketmakers demonstrate and sell their craft. Baskets and other sweetgrass items spill out in colorful displays onto the sidewalks to entice the throng of tourists visiting City Market daily.

If you linger long enough at the sidewalk displays, you'll enjoy the good-natured bantering as their nimble fingers push and pull the sweetgrass, bulrush, and pine needles into interesting designs. Charleston basketsewers are extremely leery of cameras of any kind. They quickly bow their heads, cover their faces with their hats, or walk away when they see a camera aimed in their direction. The reason, I soon found out, was that they have seen photographs of themselves in magazines, books, on postcards, and their images on television without their consent. Respecting that history, I didn't attempt to take pictures of the basketmakers themselves.

$\mathcal{P}$hilip Simmons, known affectionately in Charleston as the Gatekeeper, is a Sea Islander whose hands have created numerous iron monuments. His work is visible everywhere in Charleston, where he has made his home since 1920. He is so popular that one of his gates stands at the entrance of the Visitor's Center in Charleston. Last summer, photographs of his artistic gates were on exhibit at the Avery Research Center for African-American History and Culture (College of Charleston). The road to Mr. Simmons' success was very hard indeed. He lived with his grandparents on Daniel Island, just across the Cooper River from Charleston the first six years of his life. He credits them with teaching him good work habits and his Gullah heritage. From the time he was seven until he turned thirteen, Philip Simmons migrated between Charleston and his grandparents' home on Daniel Island. During the summers, he worked with his grandfather—farming, fishing, and shrimping. He earned enough money from these jobs to buy his own clothes to return to school in September.

In an interview with John Vlach, his official biographer, Mr. Simmons said, "I'm glad for that experience."

Philip Simmons began his career in ironwork at thirteen, but he had been intrigued by the craft much earlier. He took the long way to school each morning so he could pass the homes of the wealthy Charleston residents to see the elaborate iron gates, balconies, and railings. He admired the intricate iron designs, and would sketch them during art class.

"Tell you what get me eager to draw, because I seen so much ironwork around Charleston — the early craftsmen — and I like it. That's what get me to drawing and I do my drawing," explained Mr. Simmons in that same interview.

He said that he frequently dropped by the smithy (blacksmith's shop) on Calhoun Street to watch the activity. He loved to watch sparks fly about when the hammer met the cherry-red iron. There were four blacksmith shops owned by African Americans within a four-block radius in Charleston when Philip was a young boy, so he kept himself busy running errands and cleaning their shops. He was always drawn to ironworks, and would do any job to be close to the activity. In 1925, Philip Simmons became an apprentice under Mr. Peter Simmons (no relation), a master blacksmith. He admits that he learned the trade the hard way because Peter Simmons didn't believe in using the modern tools. During his four-year apprenticeship, Philip made horseshoes, wagons, plows, and parts for boats. He began by repairing vegetable wagons, a wheelbarrow-like wagon that people pushed around. He worked for a while with Lonnie Simmons, the son of Peter Simmons, who was also an apprentice. Lonnie dropped out because

Art in iron, wrought iron designs by Philip Simmons, at the Visitor's Center in Charleston, SC.

the work was too demanding, but Peter stayed on and was given more and more responsibility in the shop.

His pay increased with his ability. He began by sweeping the floor and putting tools away for a few pennies a day. Then he worked up to a quarter. By the end of his four years, he was earning four dollars a week.

"I was gettin' four dollars a week after become knowin' my way around and could take care of the shop by myself when the Old Man [Peter Simmons] go away," he told John Vlach. More important than the money was the knowledge he had gained from Peter Simmons. He learned how different metals responded to different amounts of heat and to different tools. He learned the best tools to use for the job and how to care for them. He learned to keep the fire "steady" for the best result, and he learned to work quickly.

I learned from people who know Mr. Simmons that he can look at a space and tell you exactly how wide it is without measuring it. He can look at a bolt and tell the diameter. His trained eye and his quick hands have gained him a place of respect in the Charleston area. Some years after he took over Mr. Peter Simmons' shop, he branched out into making gates, something that had fascinated him for a very long time. During this period, residents wanted to restore their nineteenth-century gates, and many of them contracted Philip Simmons to do it. He went from restoring gates to designing them. Philip Simmons' career as a blacksmith is an excellent example of, as Vlach said, "one craftsman's struggle to keep the past alive in the twentieth century."

Gullah descendants continue to use their creative hands to produce other crafts such as quilts, fishing nets, and dolls for their personal use and for sale.

Strip quilt, displayed at Penn Center, St. Helena, SC.

The Gullah art of quilting began with the enslaved Sea Island women who learned it from their European mistresses, particularly those of Dutch and English descent. Gullah seamstresses skillfully duplicated these European designs for their owners. At the same time, they developed the distinctive "strip" pattern for their personal use. The strip pattern is formed by sewing little strips of cloth to form longer strips from which the quilt tops were made. The strip pattern has been traced by quilting experts back to the Ashanti Kente cloth in both size of strip and color. Ashanti is a tribe in Ghana, West Africa, noted for its beautifully woven Kente cloth. Kente cloth strips are woven on "belt looms" and are about as wide as a woman's hand. So are the Gullah quilt strips.

"This relationship between Kente cloth and Sea Island quilts is part of the whole African design connection," writes Mary Twining.

Like numerous African-American women of her time, Janie Hunter learned to make quilts. Although many women were skilled in making the more detailed and ornamental quilts, most of those which survived are the simpler ones made

Man mending net using same technique as Gullah. Photograph taken in Ghana, Africa, near Elmina Castle.

Casting net, Willie Hunter, Johns Island, SC.

for their own homes. Quilts in the African-American home were meant to be functional rather than beautiful, because the main purpose for having them was to keep the family warm. However, many were functional and beautiful. Some hang in museums around the country as evidence of the skill and artistry of the African-American seamstress.

African-American women, particularly in the South, held quilting bees or parties just like their European-American counterparts. At the quilting bee women sat around a wooden "quilting frame," used to keep the fabric smooth and tight and sewed. Working from the outside to the center, the women sewed small, delicate stitches to create a design.

Mrs. Janie Hunter also sews fishing nets like the ones used by Willie Hunter in the photograph. For years, men like Willie Hunter made their living from the salty creeks, marshes, and rivers of Johns Island using nets. Making fishing nets is a carryover from West Africa where even today, men can be seen mending and sewing fishing nets. So whether Janie Hunter is making fishing nets or decorative dolls, her hands are always busy creating in the tradition of her Gullah ancestors.

Eight
A HUNDRED YEARS FROM NOW:
Holding Onto Traditions

Adusty, orange Toyota pickup barreled down the driveway leading to the Welcome Center on Daufuskie Island. It stopped abruptly in front of the gazebo which serves as the Welcome Center, leaving a cloud of dust behind it. A slightly built Black woman with a clump of sable braids pulled through the hole in her baseball cap got out of the pickup.

"Hi, I see you've met Miss Bertha," she greeted. Miss Bertha had ridden over on the boat with us from Hilton Head Island. She extended her hand and smiled broadly.

"My name is Yvonne Wilson." We shook hands and introduced ourselves.

"Mr. Jake, may I buy some gas?" she asked the aged African-American man who was tending the Welcome Center. Yvonne backed the truck about fifty feet to the pump and quickly filled up. She invited my husband, Willis, and me to sit with her in the cab of the truck so we could both hear the narrated tour.

When we first met, there was not a hint of the Gullah accent in Yvonne's speech. However, the more familiar and comfortable we became with each other the easier it was to detect the West Indian-like clip in her speech.

Yvonne was really concerned about land retention in the Gullah communities of the Sea Islands. She got really fired up about it because it is an issue which has divided the 5 by 3 1/2-mile Daufuskie Island into two opposing groups, wealthy white developers and residents on one side and poor African-American natives on the other. Developers are desperately seeking waterfront property on which to build planned communities called "plantations." These plantations,

Haig Point Welcome Center, Daufuskie Island, SC.

some of which are being developed by corporate giants, have expensive homes, stables, clubhouses, country clubs, and gorgeous 18-hole golf courses. The few African Americans left on the island are trying to hold onto their land in the face of large companies. Their way of life is rapidly being choked out by development in the same way a neglected garden is choked out by weeds.

"We have to put up with the 'reincarnation' of the plantation. It is not enough that the resorts are choking us out and forcing us off the island, but they're using a word that symbolizes so much hurt for us," Yvonne lamented as we stopped at the entrance of Melrose Plantation.

The upscale, planned communities have snuffed out the limited recreational opportunities such as fishing and crabbing for Daufuskie's African-American residents. More importantly, they have affected the islanders' means of making a living from the water which surrounds them. They can't get to it. They are cut off from the life-giving water which brought them to the Sea Islands on all sides except one. Over the years, the intracoastal waterway, the New River, and the Savannah River have been so badly polluted by industry that the shrimp, crab, and fish harvests have declined to almost nothing. Consequently, the Gullah have lost their ability to make a living from the water.

"Real estate taxes have gone up 700 percent in five years!" Yvonne exclaimed. Blacks were not told of the various tax exemptions for homesteads and agriculture until recently so they lost prime waterfront property to delinquent taxes. Yvonne learned of the exemptions through an article which was published in an Atlanta newspaper that called attention to the disparity between the amount of taxes the white landowners and Gullah landowners paid. Since then, she has gotten the needed exemptions and funds for taxes through a Land Retention Program at Penn Center on St. Helena Island. As a result of her efforts, the tax burden on Daufuskie's African-American landowners has eased.

The only jobs available to Blacks on Daufuskie are the most menial and low-paying ones. No African American is in a managerial position on the "plantations" even though they were promised such jobs. They were also promised

Coming in #2. Shrimp boats bringing in their catches, St. Helena Island, SC.

Bridge connecting Beaufort, SC, to Ladies Island, SC.

training or retraining for other responsible jobs. Five years later, developers still have not made good on their promises.

Many young people leave the island at age thirteen and never come back because there are no educational or job opportunities to keep them there. The only school on the island is the two-room Mary Fields Elementary School which was made famous by Pat Conroy's *The Water Is Wide*. Students in grades six to twelve have to get up at 5:00 A.M. to be ready in time to board the *Mary C* (school boat) at 6:30 for the ride to Hilton Head to their middle and high schools. The *Mary C* returns them to Daufuskie at 3:00 P.M. There is no such thing as an "activity" or late bus like the ones students on the mainland ride. When the *Mary C* brings them home at three o'clock, they are there until the next morning. Consequently, Daufuskie's teenagers have not been able to work part-time jobs or participate in after-school activities such as football, basketball, and cheerleading

Mary Fields Elementary School. The two-room school, made famous by Conroy's The Water Is Wide, *is still in use. Daufuskie Island, SC.*

The Mary C *school boat, Daufuskie Island, SC.*

like kids on the mainland. In the near future, though, Daufuskie's young people will finally be able to do these things, and return to the island on either the Melrose or the Haig Point boats.

This very recent development grew out of a lawsuit against Melrose Plantation by the NAACP Legal Defense Fund to remove its welcome center from a Gullah cemetery. When the final papers are signed, the cemetery, which has been designated an historic site, will be deeded to the Cooper River Cemetery Society, a Gullah organization. A positive outgrowth of the lawsuit is that Melrose Plantation has agreed to allow middle and high school students to ride the Melrose boat in the afternoons if they need to stay after school. Yvonne's teenage daughter, who is a senior in high school this year, will not have much time to enjoy the changes which have come about.

"I left Daufuskie when I was thirteen. I went to Savannah to live with a lady my mamma knew so I could go to school," Yvonne recalled. "At sixteen, my mother sent me to New York to live with my father. I finished high school and two years of college there."

Not long ago, residents could drive or walk down to the beaches which surround Daufuskie. One dirt road encircled the island and branched off to the beach on all sides. That is not true anymore. The roads don't branch off to the beaches for all residents, only the residents of the "plantations." Roads, even public county roads, have been cut off by residential communities or rerouted (with the help of the county) through areas that the county and the developers know would never be approved. To make her point, Yvonne stopped at an area which had been marked off with yellow ribbons.

"This is where they [Beaufort County] said we could build our road down to the beach, but the land they gave us runs right through protected wetlands and along a utility line. So much for cutting a road," she sighed.

At Haig Point, Yvonne showed us a double ditch which has been dug along the parameter of the Plantation, creating a giant gulf between the Black residents of the islands and the owners of resort property. So secluded are the plantations, that unless Blacks work there, they must get special permission to come through the gates.

Entrance to Haig Point Plantation, Daufuskie Island, SC.

"When I lost my baby in 1991, I had to sign a waiver stating that if anything was stolen or damaged while we were at the cemetery to bury him, I would have to pay for it." The pain of the ordeal was still evident in Yvonne's husky voice.

Another Gullah cemetery is located at the 18th hole overlooking the Atlantic Ocean at Bloody Point, the site of the massacre of the Yemassee Indians. A few feet at a time, the developer is trying to chisel away at the one-acre cemetery which belongs to Daufuskie's African-American citizens. He is being held off by a few brave residents and the NAACP Legal Defense Fund.

"What time is it?" Yvonne asked anxiously.

"11:45," I said, glancing at my watch.

"I want to show you something," she said as she picked up speed. The pickup bumped along through the deeply rutted sandy road, and she apologized for the rough ride. Soon we came to a guard gate. She whirled her truck into the driveway.

"What's this?" I asked.

"You'll see," she responded as she watched the African-American guard come from the guardhouse. They greeted each other with a familiar "hi" as he peered into the truck.

"To the cemetery," she quipped. She sat quietly as he returned to the booth to fill out the form on his clipboard.

The guard handed Yvonne the goldenrod "pass." She threw it up on the dashboard with complete irreverence and contempt, and sped down the driveway into the heart of Bloody Point Plantation.

"The only way you can get on Bloody Point is to visit this cemetery," Yvonne explained. "Any other reason, will get you thrown off."

Perhaps the greatest restriction on the Gullah people is that development has cut them off from the very water that brought their ancestors to America, the same water which has sustained them for over a hundred years. The Gullah culture is as intricately connected to the water as the Appalachian culture is to the mountains.

In light of Daufuskie's plight, Christina McNeil's statement that "A hundred years from now, we'll be doing things the same way" may not hold true for all Sea Islanders. There are some Gullah people who are struggling just to survive. Their young are leaving and their old are dying—- their numbers are shrinking.

Despite the struggle, the Gullah are aware of their responsibility to pass on to future generations the customs and traditions of their ancestors. Penn Center, the oldest school for freed slaves in America, has always taken the lead in preserving and perpetuating the Gullah culture in the United States, the Caribbean, and West Africa. It provides the organization and leadership for many outreach programs which benefit the Gullah economically and culturally. The York Bailey Museum, the Sea Island Translation/Literacy Project, the Sea Island Land Project, and the Sea Island Preservation Project are several projects which Penn Center has established to preserve the Gullah culture.

Designated a National Historic Site in 1974, Penn Center has become the oldest and most complete center for the study of Gullah culture on the East Coast. The York Bailey Museum, named for the first African-American doctor to practice in St. Helena, has the largest collection anywhere of photographs of Sea

Gravesite at Bloody Point, Daufuskie Island, SC.

Island culture, oral histories, and artifacts. It was through Penn Center that the
Sea Island Translation/Literacy Project translated the New Testament into Gullah.
Penn Center offers the only program in the state that assists African-American
and low income people in retaining their land and using it to produce income.
In addition, Penn Center conducts on-site agriculture demonstrations to teach

small farmers in the area how to get greater yield from their crops in much the same way they did in the late nineteenth century.

"I'm in school during the week," Yvonne announced during a recent phone conversation.

"That's great," I encouraged.

"Yes, I attend school at Penn Center in the Sea Island Preservation Project," she explained.

"What do you do?" I wanted to know.

"We are learning how to preserve and market our culture," she said proudly.

So Penn Center is very involved in both the cultural and economical well-being of Sea Islanders. Each November, Penn Center uses Heritage Days to raise money for the Center's many outreach programs and celebrate the uniqueness of the Gullah culture. Symposiums, lectures, tours of Penn School (Museum),

Brick Baptist Church on the Campus of Penn Center, Inc.,
where classes for freed slaves were first held.

songs, storytelling, shouts, African dancing, basketmaking demonstrations, and lots and lots of Gullah dishes are served up to thousands of eager visitors.

The celebration begins on Thursday and ends on Sunday with worship services at local churches, including historic Brick Church on the campus of Penn Center. Heritage Days provide a national audience through which the Gullah share their culture. The three-day celebration is launched with a "sing," "shouts," and spirituals. It continues on Friday with a forum which deals with subjects of interest to African Americans. On Friday night, festivalgoers enjoy an old-fashioned oyster roast and fish fry.

All types of music are performed at Heritage Days: sacred, secular, spirituals, reggae, and blues. It's interesting to watch performers draw memories from "seasoned" minds as they respond to the soulful tunes. Performances of contemporary gospel, slave songs, new arrangements of old spirituals sprinkled with storytelling revealed the range of local talent. Performer after performer proudly shared good news about themselves with their homefolk. Beaufort's own Hallelujah Singers announced that they had just signed a contract with Paramount Records to perform their unique and colorful renditions of Negro spirituals, contemporary gospel, and storytelling. Other artists arranged songs in honor of their hometown, St. Helena, and performed them for the first time at Heritage Days.

Darryl "Chill" Mitchell, co-star of the "John Larroquette Show," made a surprise appearance on stage at Heritage Days. He flew in for the day to show his support and to be with his parents who still live in St. Helena. He gave a rousing short speech on the importance of family, church, and discipline.

"We're proud people. Let's stay proud. Let's keep moving on. God bless you and I'm outta here," were Darryl's parting words to the overflowing crowd of spectators. But he wasn't "outta here" as quickly as he thought, for when he left the stage, he was immediately surrounded by a hundred eager children clamoring for his autograph.

Other heritage events like Decoration Day (Memorial Day) and Independence Day are means of showcasing Gullah culture. Even tiny Daufuskie Island has an Independence Day celebration the third weekend in June of each year.

Waiting for the parade, Penn Community Center, Heritage Days Parade,
St. Helena Island, SC.

Telling tales, lead singer/storyteller, Hallalujah Singers, St. Helena Island, SC.

African dance performed by unknown girl at Heritage Days Parade, St. Helena Island, SC.

Decoration Day is held in Beaufort, South Carolina, each Memorial Day weekend. Decoration Day dates back to the end of the Civil War when former slaves and families of Confederate and Union soliders gathered to pay homage to their heroes.

The family continues to be the largest transmitter of the Gullah culture. Families like the Hunters, the Browns, the Daises take time to teach young people the language, the songs, and the stories of their foreparents. They are also perfectly willing to share them with outsiders as well.

Sam "Papa" Brown, his daughter, Carrie Bell, and their cousins, Sadie Jenkins, Margaret Sumter, and Gloria Wright, staged an old-fashioned Gullah family gathering for my husband, Willis, photographer Gabriel Kuperminc, and myself during Heritage Days. After getting lost several times on the dark country road, we finally pulled into a neighbor's driveway to ask directions. Fortunately, someone drove up behind us and we asked him for directions.

"Follow me. I'll take you there," said the stranger.

As it turned out, he was another one of Sam Brown's cousins. We met family from Savannah and Atlanta, Georgia. We feasted on the famous "Frogmore Stew," pear cake, corn bread, chicken, and a variety of soft drinks. Then we drove a few houses down the road to Sam Brown's home, a mobile home which Carrie had enlarged into a spacious rancher. We were in for a real treat as Carrie, Papa, Gloria, Margaret, and Sadie shared snippets of their personal lives with us.

They demonstrated the Gullah handclap, lined the metered hymns in the Gullah tradition, and sang some of the spirituals which had their roots during slavery on St. Helena Island. So much of what they did was reminiscent of my own childhood where family gatherings were important.

Through his stories, the eighty-six-year-old Papa took us back to the old days on St. Helena. He told us how he plowed with a horse and remembers how he made the horse stop and go with the simple commands of "gee and haw." He proudly related how he raised enough peas, corn, rice, and sweet potatoes to feed his "eleven head of children."

Papa left St. Helena Island in 1925, at the age of eighteen, to find work as a

Sam "Papa" Brown, St. Helena Island, SC.

Carrie Bell Brown demonstrates the Gullah hand clap at her father's home on St. Helena Island, SC.

stevedore in Savannah, Georgia. He worked for a short time in the sawmill in Bluffton, South Carolina. He also worked at Parris Island for fourteen years.

"One day, I showed up at the gate [Parris Island]. In those days, if you could stand up, you could get a job," Papa said with a chuckle. "It was war time."

Papa said he was hired on the spot, but was a little scared when they asked him to take a physical exam. He finally gave in because he knew that in order to work, he had to have the physical. Parris Island provided one of the best sources of income for Sea Island men, and, since it was so close to St. Helena Island, many of the men worked there.

Of all his accomplishments, Papa is most proud of rearing his eleven children and not having to go to bail any of them out of trouble. To what does he attribute his success in child-rearing?

93

"Fireside training," he says proudly. He has always been happiest when someone came up to him and said, "Sam Brown, you got good children."

Papa is also a griot in the community. Penn Center brings the children in its summer program to his home so he can tell them Gullah stories. Papa sings the old songs in his deep, robust voice, and he shouts the old way. He is an active member of his church, and, until recently, sang with a male chorus. His picture hangs in one of the dormitories on the campus of Penn Center with other Sea Islanders who have contributed to Sea Island culture. At eighty-six years old, this remarkable Gullah man still rides the train alone to Newark, New Jersey, to stay with his daughter in the winter.

Sadie and Margaret gave us a feel for what it was like to grow up in the tightly knit Sea Island community and return to it later in life. They both agreed on one thing, they missed St. Helena and knew that one day they would return to the place they loved. A car accident changed the course of Sadie's life. She was living in Boston, Massachusetts, and was hurt on her way to work one morning. The car in which she was riding hit a tree and she was thrown out. Miraculously, she was not killed. While she was recuperating from the accident, Sadie decided

Family sing and demonstration of hand clap. Pictured, Carrie Bell Brown, Gloria Wright, Margaret Sumter, and Sadie Jenkins.

to enroll in school to get her GED. When she accomplished this goal, she went to school to become a licensed practical nurse. Sadie applied for the job of Visiting Nurse in St. Helena, and got the job.

Nowadays, Sadie Jenkins, a former visiting nurse, sits with the sick and shut-in in her neighborhood free of charge. She dreams of forming a group to provide Respite Care for the elderly caregivers in the community.

"Missionary work is my main goal and love. It's joy work," says Sadie.

Margaret finds in Sam Brown a mentor and a friend. She loves to visit him and listen to him tell stories. Her respect for him is so evident.

"Sam Brown has really influenced my life. He has taken me under his wing ever since I returned from New York," she says affectionately. "I'm an old lady, now," she chuckles. "But I still get around and try to help people."

Gloria Wright, a cousin of Sam and Carrie Bell Brown, has lived in Savannah, Georgia, all her life. The retired social worker and former teacher continues the missionary tradition of the Brown family by reaching out to youth and seniors in her community. As a retiree, she tutors children in reading, takes children to the doctor, and tries to get medical attention and supplies for the elderly in her church. She had just recently gotten a walker for an old lady. Gloria is very artistic. She arranges flowers, decorates cakes, and makes crafts.

"I've had some of my crafts at Heritage Days," she said. When asked if she had anything there this year, she replied, "Oh, no. I'm getting too old for that." But she wasn't too old to help Carrie prepare "Frogmore Stew" for the family gathering.

Carrie Bell Brown has made Papa very proud. It is because of his influence that she has been so successful. She bristles when people stereotype the roles of men and women.

"When people say women are more nurturing than men, I have to take exception. My dad was far more nurturing than my mother. He was the one who took care of the stomachaches and fevers," she said in an interview with Kristy Arnesen of *The American Baptist*. Her mother, on the other hand, was well known in the community for her business sense. Carrie Bell left St. Helena be-

Carrie Bell Brown shares her roots as Sam "Papa" Brown listens.

cause there were no "free" public high school for her to attend. She left St. Helena to attend Mather School in Beaufort and then the Baptist Missionary Training School in Chicago.

"I was blessed to attend the Mather School. It was there that I began to make 'inroads' into getting in touch with who I was," Carrie Bell said. At Mather School, Carrie Bell also came in contact with teachers who cared about her. One of those teachers was her music teacher who was instrumental in finding employment for her at Chautauqua Institute in Chautauqua, New York.

"There, I was exposed to the symphonies, operas, and plays of the best quality. I heard lectures by outstanding people, including the late Justice Thurgood Marshall," Carrie related.

As a student at Mather School, Carrie Bell was chosen to receive a scholarship from the American Baptist women in her junior and senior years of high school. She dreamed of going to school in Chicago, but she knew her parents didn't have the money to send her.

"I prayed and dreamed about attending the Baptist Missionary Training School in Chicago. I was discouraged by a teacher from attending that school because she felt that I would not 'fit' into that setting." Carrie felt very strongly that what the teacher was really saying was that a girl from the Sea Islands was not "cultured" enough to go to school with all those white girls. But she did go! With the help of the American Baptist women from Southern California and Kansas, she received the $800 yearly tuition. Her parents only had to contribute $80 the entire four years.

Carrie Bell received her Masters of Education in Guidance and Counseling from Bradley University in Peoria, Illinois. She has also done post-graduate work at Bradley and the Colgate Rochester Divinity School in Rochester, New York. Carrie Bell has been a commissioned missionary for thirty-three years and is awaiting ordination in the American Baptist Denomination. Her affiliation with the American Baptist has taken her all over the country, speaking to groups and congregations. Her main focus is on youth, and she has used her counseling skills to assist youth in conflict resolution and peacemaking. As Director of the Dayton Christian Center, Carrie Bell is working to try to stem the tide of crimes committed by youth in the area. Anyone who knows Carrie Bell Brown, knows that she gets things done when others give up.

$\mathcal{A}$ couple of summers ago, I had the good fortune of attending an exhibition of Jonathan Green's paintings at the McKissick Museum on the campus of the University of South Carolina. I was struck by the vibrancy and familiarity of his subjects. As I moved from painting to painting, I understood why he had been described in the Museum's brochure as a "master storyteller whose work draws upon the African oral traditions." His vibrant stories on canvas, more than a 150 of them, tell the story of the Gullah culture as Green remembers it growing up in the Low Country in the 1960s. The praise house, waterways, boatmen, sweetgrass baskets, shouts, storytelling, and church gatherings are themes which he expertly and vividly portrays in his paintings. Each painting has a personal story to accompany it, and, as such, his work has been labeled "narrative paintings."

Jonathan Green remembers how his maternal grandmother taught him the Gullah language. He recollects how she passed on to him the oral tradition of the Gullah through the Brer Rabbit and Dr. Buzzard tales. He appreciates and capitalizes on his uniqueness because he remembers his grandmother telling him that he was born with a "veil" over his eyes, a sign of specialness in the African-American community. Although he has lived in Chicago, New York, and traveled throughout the United States and Europe, the memory of what his grandmother taught him appears to have had a lasting effect on him. While he hasn't lived with his grandmother in Garden Corner, South Carolina, since he was a teenager, he is preserving the images of his childhood on canvas as though he were still there.

"What is seen in my work comes from a time and place, but it speaks to all times, all places and to all mankind," says Jonathan Green in an article written about him and his work in *American Visions*.

The Gullah are resilient, astute, hard-working, spiritual, intuitive, and loving African Americans who realize that they have a unique culture, and, I am confident that they will work as hard as their forefathers to keep the legacy alive for the next hundred years and more.

Bibliography

BOOKS

Aptheker, Herbert. *American Negro Slave Revolts*. Millwood, NY: Kraus Reprint, 1978.

Blassingame, John. *The Slave Community: Plantation Life in the Ante-Bellum South*. New York: Oxford University Press, 1979.

Botkin, B. A. *Lay My Burden Down: A Folk History of Slavery*. Athens, GA: University of Georgia Press, 1945.

Botume, Elizabeth H. *First Days Amongst the Contrabands*. New York: Arno Press, 1968.

Brewer, John Mason. *American Negro Folklore*. Chicago: Quandrangle Books, 1968.

Carawan, Guy, Candie Carawan and Robert Yellin. *Ain't You Got a Right to the Tree of Life?* New York: Simon and Schuster, 1966.

Chase, Judith W. *Afro-American Art and Craft*. New York: Van Nostrand, 1971.

Cohen, Lily Y. *Lost Spirituals*. New York: Walter Neale, 1928.

Conroy, Pat. *The Water Is Wide*. Boston: Houghton Mifflin, 1972.

Creel, Margaret W. *A Peculiar People*. New York: New York University Press, 1988.

Cronise, Florence M. *Cunnie Rabbit, Mr. Spider, and Other Beef*. Chicago: Afro-AM Press, 1969.

Curtin, Philip. *The Atlantic Slave Trade*. Madison, WI.: University of Wisconsin Press, 1969.

Dabbs, Edith M. *Faces of an Island*. Columbia, SC: R. L. Bryan, 1960.

Derby, Doris A. *Black Women Basket Makers*. Illinois: University of Illinois, 1980.

Doar, David. *Rice and Rice Planting in the South Carolina Low Country*. Charleston, SC: The Charleston Museum, 1936.

Donald, Henderson. *The Negro Freedman*. New York: H. Schuman, 1952.

Douty, Esther M. *Charlotte Forten: Free Black Teacher*. Champaign, IL: Garrard Publishing Company, 1971.

Dubois, W. E. B. *The Negro Artisan*. Atlanta: Atlanta University Press, 1912.

_____. *The Negro Church*. Atlanta: Atlanta University Press, 1903.

Easterby, J. H. *The South Carolina Rice Plantation as Revealed in the Papers*. Chicago: University of Chicago Press, 1945.

Edwards, Lillie J. *Denmark Vesey*. New York: Chelsea House Publishers, 1990.

Evitts, William J. *Captive Bodies, Free Spirits: The Story of Southern Slavery*. New York: Julian Messner, 1985.

Federal Writers' Project. *Lay My Burden Down: A Folk History of Slavery*. Chicago: University of Chicago Press, 1945.

Foner, Eric. *Reconstruction: America's Unfinished Revolution, 1863-1877*. New York: Harper & Row Publishers, 1988.

Genovese, Eugene D. *Roll, Jordan, Roll*. New York: Vintage Books, 1976.

Gonzales, Ambrose. *The Black Border*. Columbia, SC: The State Company, 1922.

Goss, Linda and Marian E. Barnes. *Talk That Talk*. New York: Simon & Schuster, 1989.

Hamilton, Virginia. *The People Could Fly: American Black Folktales*. New York: Knopf, 1985.

Harding, Vincent. *There Is a River*. New York: Vintage Books, 1983.

Harris, Joel C. *Nights with Uncle Remus*. Boston: Houghton, Mifflin, 1881.

Holland, Rupert S. *Letters and Diary of Laura M. Towne*. New York: Negro University Press, 1912

Johnson, Guion G. *A Social History of the Sea Islands*. Chapel Hill: University of North Carolina Press, 1930.

Jones, Charles C. *Negro Myths from the Georgia Coast, Told in the Vernacular*. Boston: Houghton, Mifflin, 1888.

Jones, Katherine M. *Port Royal Under Six Flags*. Indianapolis: Bobbs-Merrill, 1960.

Jones-Jackson, Patricia. *When Roots Die*. Athens, Georgia: University of Georgia Press, 1987.

Joyner, Charles W. *Down by the Riverside*. Urbana: University of Illinois Press, 1984.

_____. *Folk Songs in South Carolina*. Columbia, SC: University of South Carolina Press, 1971.

Kovacik, Charles F. *South Carolina: A Geography*. Boulder, CO: Westview Press, 1987.

Mbiti, John S. *Introduction to African Religion.* New Hampshire: Heinemann Educational Books, 1975.

Myers, Lynn R. *Row Upon Row: Sea Grass Baskets of the South Carolina Low-Country.* Columbia, SC: McKissick Museum, 1987.

Myers, Walter Dean. *Now Is Your Time: The African-American Struggle for Freedom.* New York, Scholastic, Inc., 1993.

Newby, I. A. *Black Carolinians: A History of Blacks in South Carolina.* Chapel Hill: University of North Carolina Press, 1930.

Opala, Joseph A. *The Gullah: Rice, Slavery, and the Sierra Leone-American Connection.* Freetown, Sierra Leone: USIS, 1987.

Parsons, Elsie Clewes. *Folklore of the Sea Islands.* Cambridge, MA: American Folklore Society, 1923.

Pearson, Elizabeth W. *Letters from Port Royal.* Boston: W. B. Clarke, 1906.

Puckett, Newbell N. *The Magic and Folk Beliefs of the Southern Negro.* New York: Dover Publications, 1969.

Rose, Willie L. *Rehearsal for Reconstruction: The Port Royal Experiment.* Indianapolis: Bobbs-Merrill Company, 1964.

Sanfield, Steve. *The Adventures of High John the Conquereror.* New York: Orchard Books, 1989.

Smith, Julia F. *Slavery and Rice Culture in Lowcountry Georgia, 1750-1860.* Knoxville: University of Tennessee Press, 1985.

Smith, Reed. *Gullah.* Columbia, SC: University of South Carolina Press, 1926.

Stampp, Kenneth. *The Peculiar Institution.* New York: Alfred A. Knopf, 1969.

Sterling, Dorothy. *Captain of the Planter: The Story of Robert Smalls.* Garden City: Doubleday & Company, 1958.

Stoddard, Albert H. *Gullah Tales and Anecdotes of the South Carolina Sea Islands.* Savannah, GA: Published by author, 1940.

Tindall, George B. *South Carolina Negroes, 1877-1900.* Columbia, SC: University of South Carolina Press, 1952.

Turner, Lorenzo D. *Africanisms in the Gullah Dialect.* Ann Arbor: University of Michigan Press, 1949.

Twining, Mary A. and Keith Baird. *Sea Island Roots: African Presence in the Carolinas and Georgia.* New Jersey: Africa World Press, Inc., 1991.

Vlach, John. *The Afro-American Tradition in the Decorative Arts*. Cleveland: Cleveland Museum of Art, 1978.

_____. *Charleston Blacksmith: The Work of Philip Simmons*. Athens, GA: University of Georgia Press, 1981.

Wood, Peter H. *Black Majority*. New York: Knopf, 1974.

Woodson, Carter G. *The History of the Negro Church*. Washington, DC: Associated Publishers, 1921.

Woofter, T. J. *Black Yeomanry: Life on St. Helena Island*. New York: Henry Holt, 1930.

Work Projects Administration. *Drums and Shadows*. Athens, GA: Georgia Writers' Project, 1940.

_____. *South Carolina Folk Tales: Stories of Animals and Supernatural Beings*. Columbia, SC: University of South Carolina Press, 1941.

NEWSPAPERS, PERIODICALS, JOURNALS, PAMPHLETS

"Beliefs and Customs Connected with Death and Burial." *Southern Workman* (26), 1897, 18-19.

Bennett, Lerone, J. "The World of the Slave." *Ebony*, April 1971, 44-56.

Blockson, Charles L. "Sea Change in the Sea Islands: No Where to Lay Down Weary Head." *National Geographic*, December 1987, 735-63.

Bradley, Francis W. "Expert View on Swamp Hants: Their Cause and Cure." *News and Courier* (Charleston, SC), January 16, 1956, 11A.

_____. "South Carolina Folklore." *News and Courier* (Charleston, SC), November 20, 1949.

_____. "Gullah Words and Sayings." *News and Courier* (Charleston, SC), December 4, 1949.

Chase, Judith Wragg. "African-American Heritage from Ante-Bellum Black Craftsmen." *Southern Folklore Quarterly*, 42(2-3), 135-138.

Chepesiuk, Ron. "The Gullah Bible: A Link Between Past and Future." *American Visions*, June, 1988, 32-36.

Cohen, Hennig, "Burial of the Drowned Among Gullah," *Southern Folklore Quarterly* (22), 1958, 93-97.

Cooley, Rossa B. "Aunt Jane and Her People: The Real Negroes of the Sea Islands." *Outlook*, October 24, 1908, 424-32.

Fitchett, E. Horace. "Superstitions in South Carolina." *Crisis*, 1936, 360-361, 370.

Forten, Charlotte. "Life on the Sea Islands." *Atlantic Monthly* (13), 1864, 587-596, 666-667.

Greene, Carroll. "Coming Home Again: Artist Jonathan Green Returns to His Gullah Roots." *American Visions,* February, 1990, 44-52.

"Hags and Their Ways." *Southern Workman* (23), 1894, 26-27.

Ingersoll, Ernest. "Decoration of Negro Graves." *Journal of American Folklore* (5), 1892, 68-69.

Jackson, Juanita, et al. "The Sea Islands as a Cultural Resource." *The Black Scholar,* March 1974, 32-35.

Manley, Howard. "An Island's Vanishing Culture." *Newsweek,* January 14, 1991, 27.

Palmer, Colin. "African Slave Trade: The Cruelest Commerce." *National Geographic,* September 1992, 62-91.

Rowe, George E. "Negroes of the Sea Islands." *Southern Workman,* 1900, 709-715.

"The Sea Islands." *Harper's* (57), 1878, 839-861.

Singleton, Vernie. "A Venture Into Shrimp: Hilton Head Island Fishing Co-op." *Southern Exposure,* November/December 1983, 48-49.

"South Carolina Gullahs Hold Ethiopian Traits." *New York Times,* January 5, 1936, Section 4, 6.

Stoddard, Albert H. "Origin, Dialect, Beliefs, and Characteristics of the Negroes of the South Carolina and Georgia Coast." *Georgia Historical Quarterly* (28), 1944, 186-195.

Thompson, Robert F. "African Influence on the Art of the United States." *Black Studies in the University: A Symposium,* Armstead L. Robinson, et al., eds. New Haven: Yale University Press, 1969, 122-170.

Williams, John. "Is Gullah a Corruption of Angola?" *Sunday News* (Charleston, SC), February 10, 1895.

Work, Monroe N. "Gechee and Other Proverbs." *Journal of American Folklore* (32), 1919, 441-442.

Index